P9-CLJ-242

PSYCHOANALYTIC TREATMENT

An Intersubjective Approach

Psychoanalytic Inquiry Book Series

Volume 8

Psychoanalytic Inquiry Book Series

Volume 1
Reflections on Self Psychology
Edited by Joseph D. Lichtenberg, M.D., & Samuel Kaplan, M.D.

Volume 2
Psychoanalysis and Infant Research
Joseph D. Lichtenberg, M.D.

Volume 3
Empathy, I & II
Edited by Joseph D. Lichtenberg, M.D., Melvin Bornstein, M.D., & Donald Silver, M.D.

Volume 4
Structures of Subjectivity: Explorations in Psychoanalytic Phenomenology
George E. Atwood, Ph.D., & Robert Stolorow, Ph.D.

Volume 5
Towards A Comprehensive Model for Schizophrenic Disorders: Psychoanalytic Essays in Memory of Ping-Nie Pao, M.D.
Edited by David B. Feinsilver, M.D.

Volumes 6 and 7
The Borderline Patient: Emerging Concepts in Diagnosis Etiology, Psychodynamics, and Treatment, 1 & 2
Edited by James S. Grotstein, M.D., Marion F. Solomon, Ph.D., & Joan A. Lang, M.D.

Volume 8
Psychoanalytic Treatment: An Intersubjective Approach
Robert D. Stolorow, Ph.D., Bernard Brandchaft, M.D., & George E. Atwood, Ph.D.

Volume 9
Female Homosexuality: Choice Without Volition – A Psychoanalytic Study
Elaine V. Siegel, Ph.D.

PSYCHOANALYTIC TREATMENT

An Intersubjective Approach

Robert D. Stolorow
Bernard Brandchaft
George E. Atwood

THE ANALYTIC PRESS
1987 Hillsdale, NJ Hove and London

Copyright © 1987 by The Analytic Press.
All rights reserved. No part of this book may be reproduced in any form, by photostat, microform, retrieval system, or any other means, without the prior written permission of the publisher.

The Analytic Press
365 Broadway
Hillsdale, New Jersey 07642

Distributed solely by
Lawrence Erlbaum Associates, Inc., Publishers
365 Broadway
Hillsdale, New Jersey 07642

Set in Goudy type by
Lind Graphics, Woodcliff Lake, New Jersey

Library of Congress Cataloging-in-Publication Data
Stolorow, Robert D.
Psychoanalytic treatment.

Bibliography: p.
Includes index.
1. Psychoanalysis. I. Atwood, George E.
II. Brandchaft, Bernard. III. Title.
[DNLM: 1. Psychoanalytic Therapy. WM 460.6 S875p]
RC504.S76 1987 616.89'17 87-12428
ISBN 0-88163-061-6

Printed in the United States of America
10

To the memory of Heinz Kohut

Contents

Preface

Our conception of psychoanalysis as a science of the intersubjective has evolved from some 15 years of collaborative work. During this time span, the concept of an intersubjective field gradually crystallized in our thinking as the central explanatory construct for guiding psychoanalytic theory, research, and treatment. As will be seen in the pages to follow, this conception of a system composed of differently organized, interacting subjective worlds is invaluable in illuminating both the vicissitudes of psychoanalytic therapy and the process of human psychological development. Our aim in this book is eminently practical—to apply our intersubjective approach to a broad array of clinical issues and problems that are critical in the practice of psychoanalytic therapy. We hope to demonstrate that adopting an intersubjective approach can greatly enlarge analysts' capacity for sustained empathic inquiry and, in the same measure, enhance the therapeutic effectiveness of psychoanalytic treatment.

This book could never have been written were it not for the landmark contributions of the late Heinz Kohut, to whom the work is dedicated. It also could not have been written without the loving support and unfailing encouragement of Daphne Socarides Stolorow, Elaine Brandchaft, and Elizabeth Atwood. Daphne Stolorow coauthored a pivotal chapter on "Affects and Selfobjects" and was of enormous help in the preparation of the entire book. Frank M. Lachmann coauthored a very important chapter on transference.

Some of the material in this book was originally published elsewhere.

An earlier version of chapter 2 appeared in *Psychoanalytic Inquiry* (1986, 6:387–402), and portions of the chapter also appeared in *Progress in Self Psychology, Vol. 2*, ed. A. Goldberg (New York: Guilford Press, 1986, pp. 273–279).

An earlier version of chapter 3 appeared in *The Annual of Psychoanalysis* (1984/85, 12/13:19–37. New York: International Universities Press).

An earlier version of chapter 5 appeared in *The Annual of Psychoanalysis* (1984/85, 12/13:105–119. New York: International Universities Press), and the clinical illustration also appeared in *Psychotherapist's Casebook*, ed. I. Kutash and A. Wolf (San Francisco: Jossey-Bass, 1986, pp. 43–54).

Portions of chapter 6 appeared in *Progress in Self Psychology, Vol. 1*, ed. A. Goldberg (New York: Guilford Press, 1985, pp. 194–201).

Earlier versions of chapter 8 appeared in *Empathy II*, ed. J. Lichtenberg, M. Bornstein, and D. Silver (Hillsdale, NJ: The Analytic Press, 1984, pp. 333–357) and in *The Borderline Patient*, Vol. 2, ed. J. Grotstein, M. Solomon, and J. Lang (Hillsdale, NJ: The Analytic Press, 1987, pp. 103–125).

We thank the editors and publishers of these journals and books for giving us permission to include this material in our book.

And, finally, we wish to express our gratitude to Paul E. Stepansky for his valuable editorial guidance, and to Lawrence Erlbaum and Joseph Lichtenberg for their enthusiastic support of this project.

1

Principles of Psychoanalytic Exploration

The essentials of an intersubjective approach to psychoanalysis were defined in our[1] earlier book (Atwood and Stolorow, 1984), *Structures of Subjectivity*:

> In its most general form, our thesis . . . is that psychoanalysis seeks to illuminate phenomena that emerge within a specific psychological field constituted by the intersection of two subjectivities—that of the patient and that of the analyst. . . . [P]sychoanalysis is pictured here as a science of the *intersubjective*, focused on the interplay between the differently organized subjective worlds of the observer and the observed. The observational stance is always one within, rather than outside, the intersubjective field . . . being observed, a fact that guarantees the centrality of introspection and empathy as the methods of observation. . . . Psychoanalysis is unique among the sciences in that the observer is also the observed . . . [pp. 41–42].
>
> [C]linical phenomena . . . cannot be understood apart from the intersubjective contexts in which they take form. Patient and analyst together form an indissoluble psychological system, and it is this system that constitutes the empirical domain of psychoanalytic inquiry [p. 64].

The intersubjectivity principle was applied to the developmental system as well:

---

[1]Throughout this book we will use the words "we" and "our" in referring to works written by one of us, two of us, or all three of us.

> [B]oth psychological development and pathogenesis are best conceptualized in terms of the specific intersubjective contexts that shape the developmental process and that facilitate or obstruct the child's negotiation of critical developmental tasks and successful passage through developmental phases. The observational focus is the evolving psychological field constituted by the interplay between the differently organized subjectivities of child and caretakers . . . [p. 65].

It is our central aim in the present book to flesh out the implications for psychoanalytic understanding and treatment of adopting a consistently intersubjective perspective. In the course of this study, the intersubjective viewpoint will be shown to illuminate a wide array of clinical phenomena, including transference and resistance, conflict formation, therapeutic action, affective and self development, and borderline and psychotic states. Most important, we hope to demonstrate that an intersubjective approach greatly facilitates empathic access to the patient's subjective world and, in the same measure, greatly enhances the scope and therapeutic effectiveness of psychoanalysis.

The concept of intersubjectivity has evolved in our thinking through a series of stages. The significance of the intersubjective perspective first became apparent to us in a study of the interplay between transference and countertransference in psychoanalytic therapy (Stolorow, Atwood, and Ross, 1978). There we considered the impact on the treatment process of phenomena arising out of the correspondences and disparities that exist between the analyst's and the patient's respective worlds of experience. An attempt was made in particular to characterize the conditions under which such phenomena may obstruct or facilitate the unfolding of the psychoanalytic dialogue. At this early stage we already were focusing on interactions between patients' and therapists' subjective worlds, but the more general concept of the intersubjective field within which psychoanalytic therapy takes place had not yet been articulated.

We then were led to an investigation of the situation that arises in treatment when there is a wide but unrecognized disparity between the relatively structured world of the analyst and an archaically organized personal universe of the patient (Stolorow, Brandchaft, and Atwood, 1983). Such a disjunction, we showed, often results in chronic misunderstandings wherein the archaic experiences communicated by the patient cannot be comprehended because of the analyst's unconscious assimilation of them to his own, differently organized subjectivity. The analyst's responses may then be experienced as grossly unattuned, precipitating a spiral of reaction and counterreaction that is incomprehensible to both parties. When the analyst fails to decenter from the structures of experience into which he has been assimilating his patient's communications, the final result is a view of the patient as an intrinsically difficult, recalcitrant person whose qualities perhaps render him unsuitable for psychoanalytic treatment. We thus had begun to understand in a very specific context how the analyst's picture of the patient's attributes crystallizes within the interplay between two personal universes.

A subsequent application of this kind of analysis to the so-called borderline personality appeared in a paper (Brandchaft and Stolorow, 1984) that forms the basis of chapter 8 in the present book. The earlier work offered a critique of the view that corresponding to the term "borderline" there is a discrete, stable, pathological character structure rooted in internal instinctual conflicts and primitive defenses. The clinical observations often cited as indicative of such defenses and conflicts were shown to be evidence of needs for specific archaic selfobject ties and of disturbances in such ties. The defining features of borderline conditions were thereby disclosed as products of a specific intersubjective situation. When a shift in this situation occurs whereby the needed understanding is felt to be present, the borderline features tend to recede and even disappear, only to return when the selfobject bond is again significantly disrupted. At that point we had recognized how the context of relatedness established between analyst and patient plays a *constitutive* role in forming and maintaining the particular psychopathological configuration that is designated by the term "borderline."

The intersubjectivity concept is in part a response to the unfortunate tendency of classical analysis to view pathology in terms of processes and mechanisms located solely within the patient. Such an isolating focus fails to do justice to each individual's irreducible engagement with other human beings and blinds the clinician to the profound ways in which he is himself implicated in the clinical phenomena he observes and seeks to treat. We have now come to believe that the intersubjective context has a constitutive role in *all* forms of psychopathology, ranging from the psychoneurotic to the overtly psychotic. This role is most readily demonstrated in the most severe disorders, wherein fluctuations in the therapeutic bond are accompanied by dramatically observable effects. In chapter 9, we offer a conceptualization of psychotic states from this point of view, with emphasis on failures of archaic selfobject ties in the specific function of validation of perception. The intersubjective context is of equal significance, however, in less severe forms of psychopathology, for example, in anxiety neuroses, depressions, and obsessional and phobic disorders. The exploration of the particular patterns of intersubjective transaction involved in developing and maintaining each of the various forms of psychopathology is in our view one of the most important areas for continuing clinical psychoanalytic research.

PSYCHOANALYTIC KNOWING AND REALITY

A basic and largely unchallenged philosophical assumption that has pervaded psychoanalytic thought since its inception is the existence of an "objective reality" that can be known by the analyst and eventually by the patient. This assumption lies at the heart of the traditional view of transference, initially described by Breuer and Freud (1893–95) as a "false connection" made by the patient and later conceived as a "distortion" of the analyst's "real" qualities that analysis seeks to correct (Stein, 1966). Schwaber (1983) has argued persuasively against this notion of transference as distortion because of its embeddedness in "a hierarchically ordered two-reality view" (p. 383)—one reality experienced by the patient and the other "known" by the analyst to be more objectively true.

A fundamental assumption that has guided our work is that the only reality relevant and accessible to psychoanalytic inquiry (that is, to empathy and introspection) is *subjective reality*—that of the patient, that of the analyst, and the psychological field created by the interplay between the two. From this perspective, the concept of an objective reality is an instance of the ubiquitous psychological process that we have termed "concretization"—the symbolic transformation of configurations of subjective experience into events and entities that are believed to be objectively perceived and known (Atwood and Stolorow, 1984, ch. 4). *Attributions of objective reality*, in other words, are *con-*

cretizations of subjective truth. Analysts' invoking the concept of objective reality, along with its corollary concept of distortion, obscures the subjective reality encoded in the patient's productions, which is precisely what psychoanalytic investigation should seek to illuminate.

A good example of this obscuring effect can be found in the persisting controversy over the role of actual childhood seduction versus infantile fantasy in the genesis of hysteria. What proponents of *both* of the opposing positions on this issue fail to recognize is that the images of seduction, *regardless* of whether they derive from memories of actual events or from fantasy constructions, contain symbolic encapsulations of critical, pathogenic features of the patient's early subjective reality.

Our view of the nature of psychoanalytic investigation and knowledge differs sharply from those of a number of other authors who, like ourselves, have been significantly influenced by Kohut's empathic-introspective psychology of the self. Wolf (1983), for example, proposes that "we oscillate between extrospective and introspective modes of gathering data" (p. 685), observing sometimes from outside and sometimes from within the patient's own subjective world. Shane and Shane (1986) argue that psychoanalytic understanding derives not only from the subjective world of the patient and the intersubjective experiences in the analytic situation, but also from "the objective knowledge possessed by the analyst of the patient's life and of human development and human psychological functioning" (p. 148). And Basch (1986) contends that psychoanalytic explanations must be grounded in experimentally validated, objectively obtained knowledge of brain functioning.

In contrast with these views, our own perspective incorporates and seeks to push to its limits Kohut's (1959) proposition that the empirical and theoretical domains of psychoanalysis are defined and demarcated by its investigatory stance of empathy and introspection. Accordingly, anything that is not *in principle* accessible to empathy and introspection does not properly fall within the bounds of psychoanalytic inquiry.

Thus, unlike Wolf (1983) we hold that psychoanalytic investigation is *always* from a perspective within a subjective world (the patient's or analyst's); it is always empathic or introspective. When an analyst reverts to experience-distant formulations (a frequent, inevitable, and often countertransference-motivated occurrence), or insists that his formulations possess objective truth, he is not operating in a psychoanalytic mode, and it is essential for the analyst to consider the impact of this shift in perspective on the analytic dialogue.

Unlike Shane and Shane (1986), we do not believe that the analyst possesses any "objective" knowledge of the patient's life or of human development and human psychological functioning. What the analyst possesses is a subjective frame of reference of his own, deriving from a multiplicity of sources and formative experiences, through which he attempts to organize the analytic data into a set of coherent themes and interrelationships. The analyst's frame of reference must not be elevated to the status of objective fact. Indeed, it is essential that analysts continually strive to expand their reflective awareness of their own unconscious organizing principles, including especially those enshrined in their "objective knowledge" and theories, so that the impact of these principles on the analytic process can be recognized and itself become a focus of analytic investigation.

In light of the foregoing discussion, it will come as no surprise that we are in fundamental disagreement with Basch's (1986) belief that psychoanalytic explanations must be grounded in a knowledge of brain functioning. We contend that brain functioning does not even fall within the domain of psychoanalysis, because it is inaccessible, in practice and in principle, to the empathic-introspective method of investigation. It is our view that psychoanalytic theory should, at all levels of abstraction and generality, remain within the realm of the experience-near. To that end, we have attempted to develop guiding explanatory constructs—such as the concept of an intersubjective field—uniquely appropriate to the empathic-introspective mode of inquiry. These constructs are concerned with organizations of subjective experience, their meanings, their origins, their mutual interplay, and their therapeutic transformation.

Goldberg (1985) has described a long-standing tension in psychoanalysis between realism, subjectivism, and relativism. That we place ourselves squarely within a subjectivist and relativist tradition is readily apparent from passages in *Structures of Subjectivity* (Atwood and Stolorow, 1984) that elucidate our conception of psychoanalytic understanding:

> The development of psychoanalytic understanding may be conceptualized as an intersubjective process involving a dialogue be-

> tween two personal universes. . . . The actual conduct of a psychoanalytic case study comprises a series of empathic inferences into the structure of an individual's subjective life, alternating and interacting with the analyst's acts of reflection upon the involvement of his own personal reality in the ongoing investigation [p. 5].
>
> The varied patterns of meaning that emerge in psychoanalytic research are brought to light within a specific psychological field located at the point of intersection of two subjectivities. Because the dimensions and boundaries of this field are intersubjective in nature, the interpretive conclusions of every case study must, in a very profound sense, be understood as *relative* to the intersubjective context of their origin. The intersubjective field of a case study is generated by the interplay between transference and countertransference; it is the environment or "analytic space" . . . in which the various hypotheses of the study crystallize, and it defines the horizons of meaning within which the truth-value of the final interpretations is determined. An appreciation of this dependence of psychoanalytic insight on a particular intersubjective interaction helps us to understand why the results of a case study may vary as a function of the person conducting it. Such variation, an anathema to the natural sciences, occurs because of the diverse perspectives of different investigators on material displaying an inherent plurality of meanings [p. 6].

Thus, the reality that crystallizes in the course of psychoanalytic treatment is an *intersubjective reality*. This reality is not "discovered" or "recovered," as is implied in Freud's (1913) archeological metaphor for the analytic process. Nor, however, would it be entirely accurate to say that it is "created" or "constructed," as some authors have claimed (Hartmann, 1939; Schafer, 1980; Spence, 1982). Rather, subjective reality becomes *articulated* through a process of empathic resonance. The patient comes to analysis with a system of developmentally preformed meanings and organizing principles, but the patterning and thematizing of his subjective life is prereflectively unconscious (Atwood and Stolorow, 1984, ch. 1). This unconscious organizing activity is lifted into awareness through an intersubjective dialogue to which the analyst contributes his empathic understanding. To say that subjective re-

psychoanalytic process

ality is articulated, rather than discovered or created, not only acknowledges the contribution of the analyst's empathic attunement and interpretations in bringing these prereflective structures of experience into awareness. It also takes into account the shaping of this reality by the analyst's organizing activity, because it is the analyst's psychological structures that delimit and circumscribe his capacity for specific empathic resonance. Thus analytic reality is "old" in the sense that it existed before as an unarticulated potential, but it is also "new" in the sense that, prior to its entrance into an empathic dialogue, it had never been experienced in the particular articulated form that comes into being through the analytic process.

We agree with Schwaber (1983) that what the analyst "knows" in the psychoanalytic situation is no more "real" than what the patient "knows." All that can be known psychoanalytically is subjective reality—the patient's, the analyst's, and the evolving, ever-shifting intersubjective field created by the interplay between them. This avowedly subjectivist and relativist position should not, however, be taken to mean that we believe that any psychoanalytic interpretation or explanatory construct is as good as the next. In *Structures of Subjectivity* (1984) we argued that psychoanalytic interpretations must be evaluated in light of distinctively *hermeneutic* criteria. These include

> the logical coherence of the argument, the comprehensiveness of the explanation, the consistency of the interpretations with accepted psychological knowledge, and the aesthetic beauty of the analysis in disclosing previously hidden patterns of order in the material being investigated [pp. 5–6].

With regard to evaluating theoretical ideas, we suggest the following criteria: (1) Does a psychoanalytic framework permit greater inclusiveness and generality than previous ones? Does it encompass domains of experience mapped separately by earlier, competing theories, so that an enlarged and more unified perspective becomes possible? (2) Is the framework self-reflexive and self-corrective? Does the theory include *itself* in the empirical domain to be explained? (3) Most important, does the framework significantly enhance our capacity to gain empathic access to subjective worlds in all their richness and diversity?

A psychoanalytic framework centering on the concept of an intersubjective field fares well by all three criteria. We intend to demonstrate in subsequent chapters (1) that an intersubjective approach can incorporate and synthesize the experience-near insights of both conflict psychology and psychoanalytic self psychology into a broader, more inclusive framework; (2) that a theory of intersubjectivity is inherently self-reflexive and potentially self-corrective, because it always includes a consideration of the impact of the observer *and his theories* on what is being observed; and (3) that the concept of an intersubjective field is a theoretical construct precisely matched to, and uniquely facilitative of, the empathic-introspective mode of investigation. Thus, we hope to convey how an intersubjective perspective can extend our capacity for empathic understanding to widening spheres of human experience.

BASIC PRINCIPLES

It is our view that two overarching principles guide the conduct of psychoanalytic treatment in all its phases and vicissitudes. The first maintains that the fundamental goal of psychoanalytic therapy is the unfolding, illumination, and transformation of the patient's subjective world. The second asserts that the transformational processes set in motion by the analytic engagement, along with their inevitable derailments, always occur within a specific intersubjective system. In this chapter we describe briefly how the basic technical precepts of psychoanalysis derive from these two cardinal principles, leaving detailed illustrations for subsequent chapters.

The Analytic Stance

The analytic stance has traditionally been defined in terms of some concept of neutrality, which is usually roughly equated with the "rule of abstinence"—the analyst must not offer his patients any instinctual satisfactions (Freud, 1919). This technical injunction derived from the theoretical assumption that the primary psychopathological constellations with which psychoanalysis was concerned were products of repressed instinctual drive derivatives. Gratification, according to this thesis, interfered with the goals of bringing the repressed instinctual wishes into consciousness, tracking their genetic origins, and ultimately achieving their renunciation and sublimation. Following

Kohut (1971, 1977, 1984), we have found that the central motivational configurations mobilized by the analytic process are not pathological drive derivatives but thwarted and arrested developmental strivings. A stance demanding the repudiation of such strivings in the service of "maturity" repeats and further entrenches the original developmental derailments (Stolorow and Lachmann, 1980).

Adopting an intersubjective perspective makes it immediately apparent that abstinence—the purposeful frustration of the patient's wishes and needs—could never be experienced by the patient as a neutral stance. Indeed, relentless abstinence on the part of the analyst can decisively skew the therapeutic dialogue, provoking tempestuous conflicts that are more an artifact of the therapist's stance than a genuine manifestation of the patient's primary psychopathology. Thus, an attitude of abstinence not only may fail to facilitate the analytic process; it may be inherently inimical to it (Wolf, 1976). We would therefore replace the rule of abstinence with the precept that the analyst's interventions should, as much as possible, be guided by an ongoing assessment of what is likely to facilitate or obstruct the unfolding, illumination, and transformation of the patient's subjective world. Such assessments require careful analytic investigation of the specific meanings that the analyst's actions or nonaction come to acquire for the patient.

What stance on the part of the analyst is most likely to create an intersubjective context in which the unfolding, illumination, and transformation of the patient's subjective world can be maximally achieved? We believe that such a stance is best conceptualized as an attitude of *sustained empathic inquiry*—an attitude, that is, that consistently seeks to comprehend the meaning of the patient's expressions from a perspective within, rather than outside, the patient's own subjective frame of reference (Kohut, 1959).

Like the rule of abstinence, the empathic stance decisively shapes the therapeutic dialogue, but in an entirely different direction. Sustained empathic inquiry by the analyst contributes to the formation of an intersubjective situation in which the patient increasingly comes to believe that his most profound emotional states and needs can be understood in depth. This, in turn, encourages the patient to develop and expand his own capacity for self-reflection and at the same time to persist in articulating ever more vulnerable and sequestered regions of his subjective life. Equally important, it progressively establishes the analyst as an understanding presence with whom early unmet needs can be revived and aborted developmental thrusts reinstated. The attitude of sustained empathic inquiry is central in establishing, maintaining, and continually strengthening the selfobject transference bond with the analyst (Kohut, 1971, 1977, 1984)—an essential ingredient of the psychological transformations that constitute therapeutic change. This strengthening is especially likely to occur when inquiry is extended to realms of experience that the patient believes are threatening to the analyst (Brandchaft, 1983).

This formulation of the empathic stance and its impact on the analytic process renders the traditional concept of a therapeutic or working alliance (Greenson, 1967; Zetzel, 1970) as an extratransference phenomenon unnecessary.[2] What formerly have been considered manifestations of a working alliance can, from an intersubjective vantage point, be understood in terms of the specific transference bond that becomes established in consequence of the patient's consistent experience and expectation of being understood. Similarly, the assumption of an absence of a working alliance is replaced by the investigation of disruptions of the transference tie.

Sustained empathic inquiry into the patient's subjective reality promotes the unhampered unfolding of patterns of experience reflecting structural weakness, psychological constriction, early developmental derailment, and archaic defensive activity. The illumination of these patterns occurs in concert with a developing transference bond in which preempted developmental processes are revitalized. Ordinarily, this bond undergoes transformation from more archaic to more mature forms as the analysis progresses (Kohut, 1984), with genuine collaboration between patient and analyst toward a common goal of understanding becoming an increasing possibility (Stolorow and Lachmann, 1980). This concept of a developing and maturing empathic bond must be sharply distinguished from a pseudoalliance based on the patient's compliant identification with the analyst's point of view in order to safeguard the therapeutic relationship. Such pseudoalliances are achieved at the *expense* of empathic inquiry, as cen-

[2]We are grateful to Chris Jaenicke for bringing this point to our attention.

tral experiential configurations believed to be out of harmony with the analyst's requirements are disavowed and sequestered from the analytic process.

Making the Unconscious Conscious

From an intersubjective perspective, how shall we conceptualize the time-honored aim in psychoanalysis of making the unconscious conscious? In *Structures of Subjectivity* (1984) we approached this question in our formulation of the "prereflective unconscious"—the shaping of experience by organizing principles that operate outside a person's conscious awareness:

> In the absence of reflection, a person is unaware of his role as a constitutive subject in elaborating his personal reality. The world in which he lives and moves presents itself as though it were something independently and objectively real. The patterning and thematizing of events that uniquely characterize his personal reality are thus seen as if they were properties of those events rather than products of his own subjective interpretations and constructions. . . . [P]sychoanalytic therapy can be viewed as a procedure through which a patient acquires reflective knowledge of this unconscious structuring activity [p. 36].

From this standpoint, "making the unconscious conscious" refers to the interpretive illumination of the patient's unconscious organizing activity, especially as this becomes manifest within the intersubjective dialogue between patient and analyst. We refer here to the ways in which the patient's experiences of the analyst and his activities are unconsciously and recurrently patterned by the patient according to developmentally preformed themes.

We emphasize that the patient's experience of the analytic dialogue is *codetermined* throughout by the organizing activities of *both* participants, with the analyst's organizing principles shaping not only his countertransference reactions but his interpretations and other therapeutic interventions as well. The patient's unconscious structuring activity is eventually discerned in the *meanings* that the analyst's activities—especially his interpretive activity—repeatedly and invariantly come to acquire for the patient. Thus, the patient's unconscious organizing principles become illuminated, first, by recognizing and comprehending the impact of the analyst's activities and, second, by discovering and interpreting the meanings into which these activities are recurrently assimilated by the patient. It is a paradox of the psychoanalytic process that the structural invariants of the patient's psychological organization are effectively illuminated and transformed only by careful analytic investigation of the ever-shifting flux of the intersubjective field encompassing the therapeutic dyad.

This paradoxical feature of psychoanalytic inquiry is well illustrated by the analysis of dreams. On one hand, "the dream constitutes a 'royal road' to the prereflective unconscious—to the organizing principles and dominant leitmotivs that unconsciously pattern and thematize a person's psychological life" (Atwood and Stolorow, 1984, p. 98). On the other hand, as we have previously demonstrated (Atwood and Stolorow, 1984), the meaning of dream symbols is grasped only by locating them within the specific intersubjective contexts in which they take form in the analytic dialogue.

Analysis of Transference and Resistance

Analysis of transference and resistance is central to an intersubjective approach to psychoanalytic treatment. As was implied in the foregoing paragraphs, analysis of transference, from our perspective, consists in the investigation of the manner in which the patient's experience of the analyst and his activities is recurrently and unconsciously organized according to preestablished patterns (see chapter 3). The aim of transference analysis is the illumination of the patient's *subjective reality* as this crystallizes within the intersubjective field of the analysis. Any assumptions of a more objective reality of which the transference is presumed to be a distortion not only lie outside the bounds of psychoanalytic inquiry; they constitute a pernicious obstruction to the psychoanalytic process itself.

An especially important aspect of transference analysis, emphasized by Kohut (1971, 1977, 1984) and exemplified throughout this book, is the analysis of *disruptions* of the selfobject tie to the analyst that becomes established. Such analysis seeks understanding of these ruptures from the unique perspective of the patient's subjective world—the events that evoke them, their specific meanings, their impact on the analytic bond and on the patient's psychological organization, the early developmental traumata that they replicate, and, especially important, the patient's expectations of how the analyst will receive the reactive affect states that follow in their wake. Consistent analysis of these complex disjunctive experiences, including the patient's anticipations of how the analyst will respond to their articulation, both illuminates the patterning of the patient's unconscious organizing activity and repeatedly mends and expands the ruptured selfobject tie, thereby permitting the arrested developmental process to resume.

Resistance analysis, in our view, is coextensive with the analysis of transference (see chapters 3–7). In resistance, the patient's experience of the therapeutic relationship is organized by expectations or fears that his emerging emotional states and needs will meet with the same traumatogenic responses from the analyst that they received from the original caregivers (Kohut, 1971; Ornstein, 1974). Thus, resistance is always evoked by some quality or activity of the analyst that for the patient heralds an impending recurrence of traumatic developmental failure, and it is critical for the progress of treatment that this be recognized and articulated. Resistance, in other words, cannot be understood psychoanalytically apart from the intersubjective contexts in which it arises and recedes. As we attempt to show in subsequent chapters, this basic principle holds true for any psychological product that emerges within a psychoanalytic process.

2

Reflections on Self Psychology

As is readily apparent throughout this book, our intersubjective approach to psychoanalysis owes an enormous debt to Kohut's psychoanalytic psychology of the self. Indeed, the theory of intersubjectivity might be seen as a development and expansion of psychoanalytic self psychology. Our aim in this chapter is twofold. First, by critically examining the theory of self psychology, we hope to bring the assumptions underlying our own approach more clearly into view. And second, by clarifying what we believe are the shortcomings in some of its concepts, we hope to highlight, broaden, and refine self psychology's essential contributions to psychoanalysis.

What are these essential contributions? To our minds, they are threefold and closely interrelated: (1) the unwavering application of the empathic-introspective mode of investigation as defining and delimiting the domain of psychoanalytic inquiry, (2) the central emphasis on the primacy of self-experience, and (3) the concepts of selfobject function and selfobject transference. These three principles constitute the foundational constructs upon which the theoretical superstructure of self psychology rests. The foundational pillars are essentially sound, but, as we will attempt to show, this is not necessarily true of the architecture that has been built upon them. We wish first to draw out briefly certain implications of the aforementioned basic principles of self psychology that have not received sufficient attention.

1. The empathic-introspective mode of investigation refers to the attempt to understand a person's expressions from a perspective within, rather than outside, that person's own subjective frame of reference. In his early landmark position paper, Kohut (1959) argued that this investigatory mode defines and delimits the field of psychoanalysis—that only what is potentially accessible to empathy and introspection falls within the empirical and theoretical domain of psychoanalytic in-

quiry. In making this proposal—and this has not been sufficiently recognized—Kohut took a giant step forward toward reframing psychoanalysis as an autonomous science of human experience, a depth psychology of human subjectivity (Atwood and Stolorow, 1984). Also not sufficiently recognized is the extent to which Kohut's paradigmatic step has been paralleled, complemented, and supported by the efforts of others who have attempted to free the phenomenological insights of clinical psychoanalysis from the Procrustean bed of materialism, determinism, and mechanism that was the heritage of Freud's immersion in nineteenth-century biology—most notably, the work of Guntrip (1967), Gill (1976), Klein (1976), and Schafer (1976). As we attempt to demonstrate later, certain of Kohut's later ideas are retrogressive in this respect—that is, they represent a partial return of mechanistic thinking.

Our own viewpoint fully embraces Kohut's claim that the empathic-introspective mode defines the nature of the psychoanalytic enterprise. As we stated in chapter 1, it is our belief that the concept of an intersubjective field is a theoretical construct precisely matched to the methodology of empathic-introspective inquiry. What we investigate with the psychoanalytic method are organizations of subjective experience, their origins and transformations, and the intersubjective systems formed by their reciprocal mutual interaction.

2. Following closely from its strict adherence to the empathic-introspective stance is self psychology's emphasis on the centrality of self-experience, conscious and unconscious, in both psychological development and pathogenesis. A singularly important implication of this emphasis, which Kohut did not address directly, is that it leads inevitably to a theoretical shift from the motivational primacy of instinctual drive to the motivational primacy of *affect* and affective experience (see Basch, 1984, 1985; Stolorow, 1984b). It is in the illumination of affective development and its derailments in an intersubjective matrix that self psychology's most significant theoretical contributions may ultimately lie (see chapter 5).

3. It is often forgotten that the term *selfobject* does not refer to environmental entities or caregiving agents—that is, to people. Rather, it designates a class of psychological *functions* pertaining to the maintenance, restoration, and transformation of self-experience. The term *selfobject* refers to an object *experienced subjectively* as serving certain functions—that is, it refers to a *dimension* of experiencing an object

(Kohut, 1984, p. 49), in which a specific bond is required for maintaining, restoring, or consolidating the organization of self-experience.[1] This concept is of enormous *clinical* importance because, by illuminating the developmental dimension of the *transference*, it permits therapists to treat patients with severe developmental arrests psychoanalytically. Once an analyst has grasped the idea that his responsiveness can be experienced subjectively as a vital, functional component of a patient's self-organization, he will never listen to analytic material in quite the same way.

All three of these closely interrelated fundamental principles contribute to making self psychology, as a theoretical framework, exquisitely self-reflexive and potentially self-corrective. For example, the conceptualization of selfobject functions and of the effect of their presence or absence on a person's self-experience alerts us to the continual impact of the observer *and his theories* on what is being observed. Put slightly differently, the consistent application of the empathic-introspective mode not only to the psychological phenomena being studied but also to the theoretical ideas that guide our observations provides us with an ongoing basis for critically evaluating, refining, expanding, and, when necessary, discarding these theoretical constructs. This, indeed, is the aim of this chapter—to apply a fundamental tenet of self psychology (that psychoanalysis should be defined and delimited by the empathic-introspective mode) to a critique of certain components of self psychological theory.

THE SUPRAORDINATE BIPOLAR SELF

Paradoxically, the concept of the "self" is without a doubt the most problematic one in the theory of self psychology. A conceptual imprecision that has pervaded the self psychology literature since the *Restoration of the Self* (Kohut, 1977) is the use of the term *self* to refer both to

[1]Similarly, the phrase *selfobject failure* does not refer to objectively assessed shortcomings of a caregiving agent but to a subjectively experienced absence of requisite selfobject functions. We prefer the phrase *selfobject failure* to the commonly used *empathic failure* because, as applied to the psychoanalytic situation, the former more clearly designates a subjective experience of the patient in the transference. Misunderstandings on the part of the analyst may or may not be experienced as selfobject failures, depending on their specific transference meanings for the patient.

a psychological structure (an organization of experience) and an existential agent (an initiator of action). In *Structures of Subjectivity* (1984), we addressed this problem as follows:

> While "personality" and "character" are extremely broad concepts pertaining to the overall structure of a subjective universe, *self* is a more delimited and specific term referring to the structure of a person's experience to himself. The self . . . is a psychological structure through which self-experience acquires cohesion and continuity, and by virtue of which self-experience assumes its characteristic shape and enduring organization. We have found it important to distinguish sharply between the concept of the self as a psychological structure and the concept of the *person* as an experiencing subject and agent who initiates action. Whereas the self-as-structure falls squarely within the domain of psychoanalytic investigation, the ontology of the person-as-agent, in our view, lies beyond the scope of psychoanalytic inquiry [p. 34].

"Psychoanalysis," we argued, "can only illuminate the *experience* of personal agency or its absence in specific contexts of meaning" (p. 34). This is because only the experience is accessible to empathy and introspection.

Some of the theoretical difficulties that follow from a failure to distinguish between the self-as-structure and the person-as-agent can be illustrated by the following sentence, typical of many that appear in the literature of self psychology: "The fragmented self strives to restore its cohesion." Here the term *self* has two distinctly different referents: (1) on the one hand, an organization of experience (called the self) has undergone fragmentation, and (2) an existential agent (unfortunately also called the self) is performing actions to restore cohesion to that organization of experience. This creates a theoretical conundrum. Clearly, it is not the pieces of something (fragments of a self) that strive toward a goal (restoration). More importantly, the second usage of self as an existential entity transforms the personal, agentic "I" into a reified "it," not unlike the id, ego, and superego of classical theory. This problem can be minimized if we restrict the concept of self to describe organizations of experience and use the term *person* (an irreducible ontological construct that falls outside the domain of empathic-introspective inquiry) to refer to the existential agent who initiates actions. With this distinction in mind, our illustrative sentence can be reworded as: "The person whose self-experience is becoming fragmented strives to restore his sense of self-cohesion."

From the standpoint of an outside observer, all of our patients are continually performing actions. However, our concern, from an empathic-introspective vantage point, is whether or not they *experience* themselves as abiding centers of initiative. This experience of personal agency, which is a basic constituent of a firmly consolidated self-organization, is a primary focus of psychoanalytic investigation for many patients. As analysts, we concern ourselves with the ontogenesis of the *sense* of personal agency, with early obstructions in this development, and with the reinstatement of the derailed structuralization processes in the transference configurations that become established.

The distinction between person and self enables us to separate conceptually the various functional capacities acquired by the person from the corresponding reorganizations and structuralizations of his self-experience. The relationship between the acquisition of functional capacities and the structuralization of self-experience can then be studied empirically. For example, how does the presence or absence of the ability to perform certain actions (the person's functional capacities) affect the development of the sense of personal agency (a constituent of the self-organization)? Contrariwise, how do consolidations or faulty structuralizations of the sense of personal agency affect the person's capacity to initiate various actions? Again we wish to stress that from an empathic-introspective perspective, our interest is in the structuralization of experience and not the acquisition of abilities as judged by an outside observer, a distinction that is often blurred in self psychological writings.

Having clarified the essential distinction between self and person, let us now examine Kohut's specific conceptualization of the bipolar self. According to this formulation (Kohut, 1977), the self is composed of two basic constituents—nuclear ambitions and guiding ideals—deriving from the developmental transformation and internalization of mirroring and idealizing selfobject functions, respectively. An abiding flow of psychological activity is said to establish itself between these two poles of the self, described metaphorically as a "tension arc." This tension arc is seen as the source of motivation for a person's basic pursuits in life.

There are several difficulties with this conceptualization. First, there is the problem of reification, which we discussed earlier, whereby the poles of the self become ossified entities that belie the organic fluidity of human experience. Second, the concept of a tension arc as a motivational construct seems to us to represent a retrogression to mechanistic thinking, reminiscent of the libidinal hydraulics of classical drive theory. Tension arcs, like drives, are not accessible to empathy and introspection (Kohut, 1959). From an empathic-introspective viewpoint, ambitions and ideals can be conceptualized as systems of affective *meanings* that are intrinsically motivational, making the concept of a tension arc unnecessary.

Perhaps most important, the assumption of an inevitably bipolar structure for the self—or of a tripolar one, as in Kohut's last theoretical work (1984)—unnecessarily narrows the vast array of selfobject experiences that can shape and color the evolution of a person's self-organization. We suspect that a great variety of selfobject functions and corresponding structural configurations of the self remain yet to be discovered by analysts whose empathic-introspective efforts are guided by differently situated points of view. Kohut (1983) alluded to this himself when he remarked: "We realize, moreover, what an enormous field for further research has opened up before us, challenging us to bring further order to an almost overwhelming range of explanatory possibilities . . . " (pp. 401–402).

In an effort in this direction, we offer in chapter 5 an expansion and refinement of the selfobject concept in which we propose that selfobject functions pertain most fundamentally to the integration of affect into the organization of self-experience, and that the need for selfobject ties pertains most centrally to the need for attuned responsiveness to affect states in all phases of the life cycle. The experience of such attunement contributes vitally to the ongoing process of self-differentiation (chapter 4) and to the consolidation of a belief in the validity of one's own perceptual reality (chapter 9).

Clinically, an expanded conception of selfobject function and selfobject transference enables us to work psychoanalytically with very archaic borderline and psychotic states previously thought by many, including Kohut (1971), to be inaccessible to such treatment (see chapters 8 and 9). What we wish to stress here is that a broadened concept of selfobject function corresponds to a more richly variegated and idiographic conception of the structure of the self. Consistent application of the empathic-introspective mode leads us away from the assumption of bi- or tripolarity and toward an appreciation of the multidimensionality of the self deriving from a multiplicity of selfobject experiences at various levels of psychological organization.

In what sense can this "multidimensional self," as we have conceptualized it, be characterized as supraordinate? Should we picture it as supraordinate to a mental apparatus, as Kohut (1977) suggested? Such a suggestion, in our view, represents another return of mechanistic thinking. The concept of the self and the concept of a drive-discharge apparatus exist on entirely different theoretical planes (Stolorow, 1983), with only the former being accessible to empathy and introspection.[2] From an empathic-introspective perspective, the metapsychological problem of the supraordinance of the self becomes transformed into a set of clinically crucial empirical questions concerning the degree to which a firmly demarcated sense of self predominates in the organization of a person's subjective experiences.

SELF-FRAGMENTATION AND DISINTEGRATION PRODUCTS

From an empathic-introspective vantage point, the term *fragmentation* can only refer to disturbances in various structural properties of a person's self-experience—for example, disruptions in the sense of self-coherence, self-continuity, or self-esteem (Stolorow and Lachmann, 1980). With this in mind, let us consider Kohut's (1977) proposition that isolated drive manifestations are "disintegration products" produced by a breakup of the cohesive self in the context of selfobject failure. As with the concept of the bipolar self, there are several difficulties with this formulation. First, as Kohut (1959) himself persuasively demonstrated, drives, as biological forces inaccessible to empathy and introspection, have no place at all in psychoanalytic theory, least of all in self psychology. We believe that what Kohut referred to as isolated drives are best conceptualized as reactive *affect* states, such as erotic lust and narcissistic rage (Jones, 1985; Stolorow, 1986a).

[2]It is for this reason that a self theory and a mental-apparatus theory could never, contrary to Kohut's (1977) proposal, exist in a complementary relationship to one another.

Second and more important, the idea of a disintegration product has a mechanistic quality that obscures the *meanings* and *purposes* of these reactive states for the experiencing person in specific intersubjective contexts. As Kohut (1971) and others (Goldberg, 1975; Stolorow and Lachmann, 1980) have shown, lustful feelings and strivings can serve the purpose of self-restoration through the search for an eroticized replacement for a missing or unsteady selfobject experience. Similarly, rage and vengefulness in the wake of injuries can serve the purpose of revitalizing a crumbling but urgently needed sense of power and impactfulness (Kohut, 1972; Stolorow, 1984a). In such instances, sexual and aggressive enactments serve to concretize and thereby solidify endangered or fragmenting structures of experience (Atwood and Stolorow, 1984, ch. 4).

In neglecting such meanings and purposes, the concept of disintegration products blurs the important clinical distinction between reactive sexual*ized* and aggressiv*ized* transference configurations, on the one hand, and primary sexual and "aggressive" transferences, on the other. The former refers to situations, as described above, in which erotic or hostile feelings pervade the transference in consequence of anticipated or experienced injuries or selfobject failures. The latter, by contrast, describes situations in which the patient is attempting, however fearfully and conflictually, to present newly emerging sexual or assertive/competitive aspects of the self to the analyst in the hope that these will be recognized as developmental achievements and affirmed (Stolorow and Lachmann, 1980). Clearly, this distinction holds critical implications for the framing of transference interpretations.

OPTIMAL FRUSTRATION AND TRANSMUTING INTERNALIZATION

Throughout his major theoretical writings, Kohut (1971, 1977, 1984) conceptualized the formation of psychological structure, both in early development and in psychoanalytic treatment, as a process whereby "optimal frustration" leads to "transmuting internalization." The most detailed account of this process as it was believed to occur in the working through of selfobject transferences appeared in *The Analysis of the Self* (1971). There it was formulated within the mechanistic assumptions of classical drive theory: Repeated interpretation of the patient's experiences of optimal frustration by the narcissistically invested selfobject was thought to result in a process of fractionalized withdrawal of narcissistic cathexes from the object and a concomitant redeployment of these cathexes in the gradual formation of particles of psychic structure, which then exercise the functions that heretofore had been performed by the object. In *The Restoration of the Self* (1977) Kohut, with a few notable exceptions, dispensed with such mechanistic constructions and framed his formulations in terms of a developmental phenomenology of self-experience. However, the implications of this theoretical shift for reconceptualizing the process of psychological structure formation were never worked out.

Careful study of Kohut's descriptions of transmuting internalization indicates that the concept combines and amalgamates two developmental processes which, as we suggested earlier in discussing the bipolar self, should be more sharply distinguished. One process involves the patient's gradual acquisition of *functional capacities* (such as self-soothing, self-comforting, and self-empathy) that he had formerly relied upon the selfobject tie to the analyst to provide. In referring to the patient's acquisition of these capacities as "internalizations," Kohut adopted Hartmann's (1939) conception of internalization as a process through which autonomous self-regulation replaces regulation by the environment. Schafer (1976) has demonstrated persuasively that to call this process "internalization" introduces misleading physicalistic and spatial reifications and that the development of self-regulatory capacities may be more adequately conceptualized in nonspatial terms. This developmental process, however, may be *experienced* as a reorganization of intersubjective space, whereby the analyst's selfobject functions become enduring features of the patient's own self-experience. Here the term *internalization* may be correctly applied.

The second developmental process embedded in Kohut's concept of transmuting internalization pertains to the *structuralization of self-experience*. Empathic-introspective reflection reveals that such structuralization need not take place solely, or even primarily, through a process of internalization. The analyst's consistent acceptance and empathic understanding of the patient's affective states and needs regularly come to be experienced by the patient as a *facilitating medium* reinstating developmental processes of self-articulation and self-demarcation that had been aborted and arrested during the formative years (see chapter 4). Thus certain articulations and structuralizations of self-experience are directly promoted in the medium of the analyst's empathy, a process that need not include internalization per se. Furthermore, an understanding of these developmental processes does not require any assumption about optimal frustrations providing their motivational fuel.[3]

The idea of optimal frustration as the basis for structure formation is a remnant of drive theory and its quantitative metaphors, which persisted throughout Kohut's theorizing. It is a direct descendant of Freud's (1923) proposal that "the ego is that part of the id which has been modified by the direct [frustrating] influence of the external world" (p. 25). As a mechanistic, experience-distant concept, the notion of optimal frustration is incompatible with an empathic-introspective psychology of the self (Stolorow, 1983).

The clinical observations that the theory of optimal frustration/transmuting internalization was designed to explain concerned the undeniable therapeutic benefit of analyzing ruptures in selfobject transference bonds. The therapeutic action of such analysis, we believe, lies in the integration of the disruptive affect states that such ruptures produce and in the concomitant mending of the broken selfobject tie. Structure formation, we are contending, occurs primarily when the bond is *intact* or in the process of becoming restored. The selfobject transference tie is thus seen as an archaic intersubjective context in which the patient's derailed psychological growth is permitted to resume, in the medium of the analyst's understanding. This experience-near explanation, compatible with the empathic-introspective mode, replaces "optimal frustration" with some conception of "optimal empathy" (Stolorow, 1983) or "optimal responsiveness" (Bacal, 1985) and the centrality of affect attunement (see chapter 5).

FALSE DICHOTOMIES

From Kohut's early papers on narcissism (1966, 1968) to his final theoretical statement (1984), human subjective worlds have been pictured as populated by two distinct types of psychological objects—selfobjects, experienced as part of oneself and/or serving to maintain the organization of self, and "true" objects, firmly demarcated from oneself

[3]In his third book (1984, p. 100), Kohut himself raised the question, to be answered by further psychoanalytic research, whether self-structuralizing processes can occur within a selfobject bond along pathways that require neither internalization nor frustration.

and targets of passionate desire. Such dualities, like all typological systems, lend themselves to the irresistible temptation to substantialize the products of human thought, transforming psychological categories into static, immutable entities—reifications that necessarily obscure the complex, ever-shifting flux of human psychological life. These typological reifications lead inevitably to the encrustation of false dichotomies that, in turn, become sources of endless ideological controversy, as in the current heated debate over the centrality of developmental deficit versus psychic conflict in psychoanalytic theory.

The selfobject-true object dichotomy that pervades Kohut's thought originated historically in the embeddedness of his early ideas in classical drive theory. Narcissistic libido and object-instinctual energies were each thought to follow their own distinct developmental pathways, cathecting their respective targets of investment (Kohut, 1971). However, even after Kohut abandoned both classical metapsychology and the idea that selfobject relations evolve into true object relations, claiming instead that one never outgrows one's need for selfobject ties and that such relatedness undergoes development from archaic to mature modes, the essential dichotomy was still retained, forming the basis for a theoretical complementarity between self psychology and conflict psychology (Kohut, 1977). Moreover, as we pointed out earlier, statements about self-selfobject relationships, selves seeking psychological nourishment from their selfobjects, and selfobjects responding empathically to selves, all entail reifications that transform organizations of subjective experience and psychological functions into palpable entities and existential agents performing actions. Such reifications are readily seized upon by critics who would trivialize Kohut's contributions by reducing them to a prescientific soul psychology or crude interpersonalism.

These theoretical pitfalls can be avoided if we use the term *selfobject* always and only to refer to a class of psychological *functions*, a *dimension* of experiencing an object. With the aid of this conceptual clarification, empathic-introspective reflection leads us away from the selfobject-true object dichotomy and its attendant reifications toward a multidimensional view of human experience in general and of experiencing an object in particular (Stolorow, 1986b). Our listening perspective becomes thereby focused on the complex *figure-ground relationships* among the selfobject and other dimensions of experiencing another person (see chapters 3 and 7). It is in these fluctuating figure-ground relationships that the experiential meaning of Kohut's principle of complementarity between self psychology and conflict psychology can be found (Stolorow, 1985). From this perspective, selfobject failure and psychic conflict are seen not as dichotomous but as dimensions of experience that are indissolubly interrelated. Indeed, it can be shown that the formation of inner conflict, whether in early development or in the psychoanalytic situation, always takes place in specific intersubjective contexts of selfobject failure (see chapter 6).

We are suggesting that a multiplicity of such dimensions coexist in any complex object relationship, with certain meanings and functions occupying the experiential foreground and others occupying the background, depending on the subject's motivational priorities at any given moment. Furthermore, the figure-ground relationships among these multiple dimensions of experience may significantly shift, corresponding to shifts in the subject's psychological organization and motivational hierarchy, often in response to alterations or disturbances in the tie to the object. For example, the conflictual dimension invariably comes to the fore in reaction to anticipated or experienced selfobject failure.

These considerations hold critical implications for the understanding and analysis of analytic transferences. In certain transference configurations—for example, those elucidated by Kohut (1971, 1977, 1984)—the selfobject dimension is clearly in the foreground, because the restoration or maintenance of self-experience is the paramount psychological purpose motivating the patient's specific tie to the analyst. In other transference configurations, the selfobject dimension operates silently in the background, enabling the patient to confront frightening feelings and painful dilemmas.

In still other situations, the analyst is perceived as significantly failing to provide requisite selfobject functions. Here the analyst is *not* experienced as a selfobject, but as a source of painful and conflictual affect states, in turn engendering resistance. When, in such instances, the patient is resisting the emergence of central selfobject needs, it makes no theoretical sense to speak of the analytic relationship as a self-selfobject unit,[4] because the selfobject dimension of the transference has become temporarily obliterated or obstructed by what the pa-

[4] It is for this reason that we employ the more inclusive concept of an intersubjective field, because it is broad enough to encompass both the selfobject and the conflictual/resistive/repetitive dimensions of the therapeutic system (see chapter 7).

tient has perceived as actual or impending selfobject failure from the side of the analyst, and the analysis must focus on the patient's fears of a transference repetition of traumatically damaging childhood experiences (Kohut, 1971; Ornstein, 1974). When such fears or disturbances are sufficiently analyzed and the broken bond to the analyst is thereby mended, then the selfobject dimension of the tie becomes restored, either to its position in the foreground or to the silent background of the transference. The analyst's comprehension of these shifting figure-ground relationships among the selfobject and other dimensions of experience, as they oscillate between the foreground and background of the transference, should determine the content and timing of transference interpretations (see chapter 3). Indeed, it is here, in the analysis of transference, that the unwavering application of the empathic-introspective stance produces the greatest yields in both maximizing our therapeutic effectiveness and advancing our psychoanalytic theories. This, we believe, was Kohut's greatest contribution.

CONCLUSION

We have applied a fundamental tenet of self psychology—that psychoanalysis should be defined and delimited by the empathic-introspective mode of inquiry—to a critical examination of self psychological theory. Our aim has been a dual one: to clarify the assumptions underlying our own approach, and to highlight, broaden, and refine self psychology's essential contributions to psychoanalysis. We have hoped to bring this evolving framework one step closer to actualizing Kohut's goal of reframing psychoanalysis as an empathic-introspective depth psychology of human subjectivity, capable of encompassing the full richness and diversity of experience that crystallizes in the microcosm of the psychoanalytic dialogue.

3

Transference—The Organization of Experience

(written in collaboration with Frank M. Lachmann)

Of the concepts introduced by Freud to illuminate human nature, transference is the most encompassing. It occupies a pivotal position in every aspect of psychoanalysis. It is pictured as the tidal wave of the past that washes over the present, leaving its unmistakable residues. It is invoked to explain bizarre acts of aggression, painful pathological repetitions, and the tender and passionate sides of love and sex. First seen only as a resistance to psychoanalytic treatment, it was later acknowledged as its facilitator as well. Generations of analysts have sought to use transference to distinguish analyzable from nonanalyzable patients. Finally, the concept of transference has been used to disparage cures obtained by nonpsychoanalytic therapies and to excuse failures encountered in psychoanalytic treatments.

Initially, the idea of transference was applied far more modestly. Breuer and Freud (1893–95) ascribed what we now call transference to a "false connection" made by the patient. They noted that this was both frightening to the patient and a regular occurrence in some analyses, wherein the patient transferred "on to the figure of the physician the distressing ideas which arise from the content of the analysis" (p. 302).

The image of the transference "arising" was consistent with the "archeological" model implicit in much of Freud's psychoanalytic theorizing, a model based on an assumption that the patient knew everything that was of any pathogenic significance (Bergmann and Hartman, 1976). Writing twenty years later, Freud (1913) still conceived of psychoanalysis as a technique whereby one digs into the unconscious and clears ever deeper layers: Psychoanalysis "consists in tracing back one psychical structure to another which preceded it in time and out of which it developed" (p. 183).

The archeological model has retained some hold on the clinical understanding of transference in general. More specifically, the very early notion of a "false connection" has been preserved in considering transference a "distortion" of reality. Other explanations of transference as regression, displacement, and projection, though consistent with a dynamic viewpoint, still retain a residue of the colorful imagery of archeological expeditions. The archeological model shows many of the disadvantages of Freud's energy theory, in that psychological motivations and states are treated as though they were finite, palpable entities. How this has affected our understanding of transference was a central concern leading to this chapter.

Bergmann and Hartman (1976) wrote:

> Following Freud's emphasis on archeology as the model for psychoanalysis, psychoanalysts tended to see their work essentially as a reconstruction of what has once existed and was buried by repression. By contrast, Hartmann sees the work of interpretation not only, or not even primarily, as that of reconstruction, but rather as the establishment of a new connection, and therefore as a new creation [p. 466].

In contrast with the archeological viewpoint, this emphasis on new connections and new creations within the therapeutic process focuses attention on the contributions of both patient and analyst. The focus on the analyst's contribution to the analytic process, which is made explicit in our conceptualization of the psychoanalytic situation as an intersubjective system, reflects a shift in psychoanalysis and in scientific thinking in general. How we study a phenomenon affects and alters it.

We turn now to a critical examination of formulations that traditionally have been employed to describe and explain transference.

CONCEPTUALIZATIONS OF TRANSFERENCE

Transference as Regression

The traditional psychoanalytic view of transference as regression was clearly enunciated by Waelder (1956): "Transference may be said to be an attempt of the patient to revive and re-enact, in the analytic situation and in relation to the analyst, situations and phantasies of his childhood. Hence, transference is a regressive process" (p. 367).

A survey of the uses of the term "regression" in psychoanalytic writings (see Arlow and Brenner, 1964) reflects the variety of ways, each with vastly different meanings and implications, in which this concept has been applied. Included are discussions of psychosexual regression, topographic regression, structural regression, genetic regression, etc. These different terms can be assigned to two general uses of the concept—regression as a diminution in the level of psychological organization and regression as retrogression along a time dimension. No doubt archaic modes of psychological organization in adults are related to the psychological organizations found in childhood. However, these archaic modes are not identical with their manifestations and occurrences in the young child. To confine the concept of regression solely to level of structuralization requires fewer unverifiable assumptions. With respect to transference, the concurrent influences of various modes and levels of organization can be addressed, with full recognition of their complex interplay, and with no assumption of a literal retrogression in time.

The assumption that adult relationships in their repetitive and conflictual aspects are isomorphic reenactments of traumatic relationships from the early history of the individual has enabled analysts to link the current psychopathology, the course of early development including its pathological variations, and the nuances of the patient-analyst relationship, the transference. Careful observations of patients' transferences and inferences based on these have provided analysts with data for reconstructions of specific genetic sequences and for formulating an epigenetic theory. For these assumptions with respect to temporal regression to be verified, it must be demonstrated that inferences about childhood derived from adult analyses can be validated independently and that modes of mental organization characteristic of early childhood are sufficiently similar to archaic modes of organization as they emerge in adult analyses to warrant inferential leaps from one epoch in the life cycle to the other.

Major challenges to the assumption that adult psychopathology reflects temporal regressions to infantile phases of development are found in recent observations of early infancy (Brody, 1982; Stern, 1985). There is now increasing evidence that the autism of adult schizophrenic patients has no counterpart in infancy. The postulation of an autistic phase or of an undifferentiated phase is not supported by the accumulating evidence. The adult psychopathology, therefore, cannot be accurately described as a temporal regression to an earlier normal phase (Silverman, 1986). Furthermore, when it appears that the autistic adult suffered from similar states in childhood, regression is again not an appropriate term, since the state has evidently remained present all along.

Consistent with the findings from the infancy literature is the hypothesis that the infant alternates between periods of oneness with its mother, as inferred from synchronous action patterns, and periods of disengagement (Stern, 1983; Beebe, 1986). Both patterns are characteristic of the young infant; neither is primary or a precondition for the other. Adult psychopathology that is characterized by a predominance of dependent clinging to maternal figures is often described as a regression to a phase of early infancy—for example, the symbiotic phase. However, prolonged or continuous periods of symbiosis are apparently neither typical nor normative for the infant. Thus, symbiotic-like wishes or fantasies may characterize adult motivation and may be related to an early developmental period, but what the adult imagines, yearns for, or enacts is not identical to what is typical of the young child.

The idea of temporal regression is most frequently used with respect to psychosexual development. Discussions in which psychopathology is understood as a regression to oral, anal, phallic, or oedipal phases presuppose that the predominant motivational priorities of the patient are identical to those of the child in the earlier phases. There are two questionable assumptions here. The first pertains to the linearity of psychosexual development—the notion that in the adult earlier motivations are normally renounced or relinquished in favor of later ones. It is assumed that maturity requires renunciation and that, indeed, such renunciation is possible. The concept of temporal regression, therefore, implies a failure in renunciation. The second questionable assumption is that an adult whose motivations are dominated by psychosexual wishes and conflicts must be functioning like a child who is traversing the corresponding psychosexual phases.

Restricting the concept of regression to the level of psychological organization clarifies its relevance for the transference. Analysts are thereby alerted to the possibility that higher levels of organization, which include self-empathy, perspective, humor, wisdom, and differentiation between self and other, though not in evidence, can potentially be revived or achieved. Analysts can also then better assess whether more archaic organizations had previously been prematurely aborted, precluded, or disavowed, so that their emergence in treatment is a developmental achievement (Stolorow and Lachmann, 1980), or whether they serve to ward off other material. In all cases, the analytic stance toward the emergence of archaic modes of organization should be to promote their integration with other, more mature modes, thereby enriching psychological functioning, rather than to insist on their renunciation or elimination.

Included in the concept of structural regression are both defensive revivals of archaic states and the emergence in treatment of arrested aspects of early developmental phases. In neither case can the patient be said to have actually retrogressed to an infantile period. We can only say that the patient's experiences, especially of the analytic relationship, are being shaped by archaic organizing principles, either for the purpose of defense, or in order to resume a developmental process that had become stalled.

Transference as Displacement

The repetition compulsion and displacement are two closely related concepts frequently invoked to explain the occurrence of transference. To Freud (1920), the repetition compulsion, a biologically inherent attribute of living matter, provided an explanation for the ubiquity of transference phenomena. We will consider the issue of repetition later. Displacement initially referred to a mechanism of the dream-work (Freud, 1900) and neurotic symptom formation (Freud, 1916–17). According to Nunberg (1951), the patient "displaces emotions belonging to an unconscious representation of a repressed object to a mental representation of an object of the external world" (p. 1).

Assumed within this concept of displacement is Freud's economic theory–a cathexis being pushed along an associative path from an idea of greater emotional intensity to a more distant one of lesser intensity, from a place where discharge is conflictual and blocked to a place where discharge is possible. For example, hostility initially directed unconsciously toward the same-sexed parent in childhood may be displaced to a superior at work. The presumed repetitive reliving of the past in the present neither improves one's current life nor alters one's perspective on or memories of the past. On the contrary, such reliving of the past in displaced form is believed to perpetuate the archaic configuration, until it becomes engaged in the analytic transference and can be interpreted.

In our view of transference, there is nothing that is *removed* from the past and attached to the current situation. It is true that the organization of the transference gives the analyst a glimpse of what a childhood relationship was like or what the patient wished or feared it could have been like. However, this insight into the patient's early history is possible not because an idea from the past has been displaced to the present, but because the structures that were organized in the past either continue to be functionally effective or remain available for periodic mobilization. That is, these themes have either remained overtly salient throughout the patient's life prior to the beginning of treatment or have been providing a more subtle background organization which the analytic process has brought to the fore.

The concept of transference as displacement has perpetuated the view that the patient's experience of the analytic relationship is solely a product of the patient's past and psychopathology and has not been determined by the activity (or nonactivity) of the analyst. This viewpoint is consistent with Freud's archeological metaphor. In neglecting the contribution of the analyst to the transference, it contains certain pitfalls. Suppose an archeologist unknowingly dropped a wristwatch into a dig. If the assumption is made that anything found in the dig must have been there beforehand, some woefully unwarranted conclusions would be reached.

Transference as Projection

Analysts who draw upon the theoretical ideas of Melanie Klein tend to conceptualize transference as a manifestation of the mechanism of projection. Racker (1954), for example, viewed transference as the projection of rejecting internal objects upon the analyst, whereby internal conflicts become converted into external ones. Similarly, Kernberg (1975) attributes certain archaic transference reactions to the operation of "projective identification," a primitive form of projection whose main purpose is to externalize all-bad, aggressive self and object images.

We define projection as a defensive process in which an aspect of oneself is excluded from awareness by being attributed to an external object, in order to alleviate conflict and avoid danger. To view transference phenomena solely or primarily as defensive externalizations confines the explanation of transference to only one of its many possible functions and can lead to a serious neglect of its other dimensions and multiple meanings. Once the transference is established, projection may or may not emerge as a component, depending on the extent of its prominence as a characteristic mode of defense against the subjective dangers experienced at any particular juncture.

A particular difficulty with formulations of transference as an expression of projection is that they often obscure the developmental dimension of the transference. As we have stressed elsewhere (Stolorow and Lachmann, 1980), projection as a defense actively employed to ward off conflict can come into play only after a minimum of self-object differentiation has been reliably achieved. Defensive translocation of mental content across self-object boundaries requires that those boundaries have been partially consolidated. When states of confusion between self and object occur in the context of an archaic transference configuration, this developmental achievement in self-boundary formation cannot be presupposed. Such archaic transference states are most often best understood not as manifestations of projective mechanisms, but rather as remnants of developmental arrests at early modes of experience in which self and object are incompletely distinguished.

Transference as Distortion

Implicit in the conceptions of transference discussed so far (as temporal regression, displacement, or projection) is the idea that transference involves a distortion of "reality," as the relationship with the analyst becomes cast in images from the patient's unconscious infantile past or infiltrated by the patient's endopsychic world of internal object relations. This idea was made explicit in Sullivan's (1953) concept of "parataxic distortion," a process by which a present relationship is presumed to be "warped" by earlier ones. Certain Freudian authors, too (e.g., Stein, 1966), have stated more or less directly that the goal of analysis is to correct the patient's distortions of what the analyst "knows" to be objectively real.

In another context (Stolorow and Lachmann, 1980), we have cautioned against certain dangers embedded in the concept of a "real" relationship between analyst and patient, of which the transference is presumed to be a distortion. Such dangers lie in the fact that judgments about what is "really true" about the analyst and what is distortion of that "truth" are ordinarily left solely to the discretion of the analyst—hardly a disinterested party. We find that therapists often invoke the concept of distortion when the patient's feelings, whether denigrating or admiring, contradict self-perceptions and expectations that the therapist requires for his own well-being.

Gill (1982), whose views on this subject are compatible with our own, criticizes the concept of transference as distortion because it implies "that the patient is manufacturing his experience out of whole cloth" (p. 117). "A more accurate formulation than 'distortion,' " Gill argues, "is that the real situation is subject to interpretations other than the one the patient has reached . . . Indeed," he continues, "seeing the issue in this way rather than as a 'distortion' helps prevent the error of assuming some absolute external reality of which the 'true' knowledge must be gained" (p. 118). As we noted in chapter 1, Schwaber (1983) also objects to the notion of transference as distortion because of its embeddedness in "a hierarchically ordered two-reality view" (p. 383)—one reality experienced by the patient and the other "known" by the analyst to be more objectively true.

Transference, fully established, is a sampling of psychic reality in purest culture. As such, it belongs to what Winnicott (1951) called "the realm of illusion," an "intermediate area of experience, *unchallenged in respect of its belonging to inner or external reality* . . . " (p. 242, emphasis added). A prime example of this respect for illusory experience is the attuned parent's attitude toward a child's transitional object. "It is a matter of agreement between us and the baby," Winnicott wrote, "that *we will never ask the question* 'Did you conceive of this or was it presented to you from without?' The important point is that no decision on this point is expected. The question is not to be formulated" (pp. 239–240, emphasis added). One could scarcely find a better description of the proper analytic attitude for facilitating the unfolding and illumination of the patient's transference experience.

Transference as Organizing Activity: A Reformulation

In our view, the concept of transference may be understood to refer to all the ways in which the patient's experience of the analytic relationship is shaped by his own psychological structures—by the distinctive, archaically rooted configurations of self and object that unconsciously organize his subjective universe. Thus transference, at the most general level of abstraction, is an instance of *organizing activity*—the patient *assimilates* (Piaget, 1954) the analytic relationship into the thematic structures of his personal subjective world. The transference is actually a microcosm of the patient's total psychological life, and the analysis of the transference provides a focal point around which the patterns dominating his existence as a whole can be clarified, understood, and thereby transformed.

From this perspective, transference is neither a regression to nor a displacement from the past, but rather an expression of the *continuing influence* of organizing principles and imagery that crystallized out of the patient's early formative experiences. Transference in its essence is not a product of defensive projection, although defensive aims and processes (including projection) certainly can and do contribute to its vicissitudes. The concept of transference as organizing activity does not imply that the patient's perceptions of the analytic relationship distort some more objectively true reality. Instead, it illuminates the specific shaping of these perceptions by the structures of meaning into which the analyst and his actions become assimilated.

The concept of transference as organizing activity offers an important clinical advantage over the other formulations in that it explicitly invites attention to both the patient's psychological structures and the input from the analyst that they assimilate (Wachtel, 1980). As Gill (1982) repeatedly observes, it is essential to the analysis of transference reactions to examine in detail the events occurring within the analytic situation that evoke them. The transference reactions become intelligible through comprehending the *meanings* that these events acquire by virtue of their assimilation by the patient's subjective frame of reference—by the affect-laden, archaically determined configurations of self and object that pervade his psychological life.

Another advantage of the concept of transference as organizing activity is that it is sufficiently general and inclusive to embrace the multiplicity of its dimensions, the subject to which we now turn.

DIMENSIONS OF THE TRANSFERENCE

The Multiple Functions of Transference

We have suggested a reformulation of the concept of transference from one that was encumbered by the psychoeconomic viewpoint and an outdated archeological metaphor to one emphasizing the psychological process of organizing current experience. This process occurs through the continual confluence of present events and previously formed psychological structures. Thus, what shapes the experience of a current situation, including the analytic situation, is derived from a multitude of sources in the person's history, as well as from properties of the current situation and the meanings into which these are assimilated. Transference must therefore be understood from a multidimensional perspective, on the assumption that a multiplicity of thematic structures and levels of psychological organization will have been mobilized by the analysis. Different dimensions of the transference will become salient at different points in the analysis.

The concept of transference as organizing activity is an alternative to the view that transference is the manifestation of a biologically rooted compulsion to repeat the past. In addition, transference as organizing activity focuses more narrowly on the specific patterning of experience within the analytic relationship, to which both patient and analyst contribute. Thus we have used the term in two ways. As a higher order, supraordinate psychological principle, it replaces the biological repetition compulsion. Transference is conceived, not as a biologically determined tendency to repeat the past ad infinitum for its own sake, but rather as the expression of a universal psychological striving to organize experience and construct meanings.

Within the narrower focus on the shaping of the analytic relationship, the transference can subserve the entire gamut of psychological functions that have been illuminated by clinical psychoanalysis. The organization of the transference can (1) fulfill cherished wishes and urgent desires, (2) provide moral restraint and self-punishment, (3) aid adaptation to difficult realities, (4) maintain or restore precarious, disintegration-prone self and object imagoes, and (5) defensively ward off configurations of experience that are felt to be conflictual or dangerous. Viewing the transference in terms of its multiple functions enables the analyst to examine what is most salient in the patient's motivational hierarchy at any particular juncture.

The Relationship of Transference to Resistance

The relationship of transference to resistance is a complex one and has been the source of disagreements among analysts since Freud's early papers on the subject. Both Racker (1954) and Gill (1982) have pointed out that embedded in Freud's writings on transference and resistance are two distinct and contradictory theoretical models of the relationship between them. Racker's (1954) discussion of these two different viewpoints deserves quotation at some length:

> [In the first view the transference] is regarded and interpreted as a resistance to the work of remembrance, and is utilized as an instrument for remembering, but [in the second] the transference is itself regarded as the decisive field in which the work is to be accomplished. The primary aim is, in the first case, remembering; in the second, it is re-experiencing [p. 75].
>
> The two points of view may also be said to differ in that in the former transference is regarded predominantly as arising from resistance, whereas in the latter resistance is mainly a product of transference. In the first, the analysand repeats so as not to remember; in the second, he repeats defences (resistances) so as not to repeat traumatic or anxious experiences [pp. 75–76].

The first model of the relationship between transference and resistance, in which repetition is a defense against remembering, is a relic of Freud's archeological metaphor for the analytic process. As such, it should be abandoned as a theoretical and therapeutic anachronism. The second model, in which the experience of transference is central to the analytic process (Strachey, 1934; Gill, 1982), is compatible with our own conception of the transference as equivalent to the patient's organizing activity and as a microcosm providing therapeutic access to the patient's psychological world and history.

From this latter perspective, what is the relationship of transference to resistance? Gill (1982), embracing as we do Freud's second model of this relationship, claims that "all resistance manifests itself by way of transference" (p. 29) and that "the analysis of resistance is in effect the analysis of transference" (p. 39). He then proposes two broad categories of relationship between transference and resistance: resistance to the transference and resistance to the resolution of the transference. Resistance to the transference is further subdivided into resistance to the awareness of transference, as when transference feelings must be inferred from allusions to them in extratransference material, and resistance to involvement in transference.

Kohut (1971) also discussed resistance to involvement in transference, specifically describing resistances to involvement in archaic idealizing and mirror transferences. Such resistance, triggered by disintegration anxiety and the need to preserve a fragmentation-prone self, was seen by Kohut to arise from two sources. First, the patient may resist involvement in the transference for fear that his emerging archaic needs will meet with traumatic disappointments, rejections, and deprivations similar to those he had experienced as a child. Second, the patient may resist the transference, sensing his own structural vulnerabilities, as when a need for merger is fended off for fear of the extinction of individual selfhood.

An important implication of Kohut's overall viewpoint for the analysis of resistance to involvement in transference is that such resistance cannot be viewed solely in terms of isolated intrapsychic mechanisms located within the patient. Resistance to the transference based on "the dread to repeat" (Ornstein, 1974) past traumas is always to some extent evoked by actions of the analyst that the patient experiences as unattuned to his emerging feelings or needs. Such experiences of selfobject failure invariably trigger resistance because for the patient they signal the impending recurrence of traumatically damaging childhood experiences. Since resistance to involvement in transference is in part a product of the patient's organizing activity, it is actually already an expression of the transference.

Gill's second broad category of relationship between transference and resistance–resistance to the resolution of the transference–seems to us to embody an assumption that analysis seeks to enable the patient to "renounce" infantile fixations as these are worked through in the transference, and that this goal of renunciation engenders resistance. Later we shall present our objections to this notion that transference is to be resolved or renounced. In the present context we wish to stress that, in our view, the persistence of transference is not primarily the product of resistance. It is the result of the continuing influence of established organizing principles when alternative modes of experiencing the self and object world have not yet evolved or become sufficiently consolidated. We would thus replace Gill's "resistance to the resolution of the transference" with the concept of *resistance based on transference*. This would encompass all of the anticipated dangers and resulting constrictions of the patient's psychological life that appear in direct consequence of the transference having become firmly established, including those forfeitures of self-experience that the patient believes are necessary to maintain the analytic relationship. As we elaborate in detail in the chapters that follow, such resistance cannot be understood psychoanalytically apart from the intersubjective contexts in which it arises and recedes.

The Developmental Dimension of Transference

Recent advances in psychoanalytic developmental psychology have highlighted the central importance of developmental transformations in the child's organizing activity, leading to the progressive articulation, differentiation, integration, and consolidation of the subjective world. The conception of transference as organizing activity can encompass this developmental dimension as an aspect of the analytic relationship in a way that earlier concepts of transference cannot. We refer to instances in which the patient seeks to establish with the analyst a nexus of archaic relatedness in which aborted structuralization processes can be resumed and arrested psychological growth can be completed.

A major contribution to our understanding of the developmental aspect of transference was Kohut's (1971, 1977) formulation of the selfobject transferences, wherein the patient attempts to reestablish with the analyst ties that were traumatically and phase-inappropriately ruptured during the formative years, and upon which he comes to rely once again for the restoration and maintenance of the sense of self. We have come to believe that it has been a conceptual error to consider the term *selfobject transference* to refer to a *type* of transference characteristic of a certain type of patient. Instead, we now use the phrase *selfobject transference* to refer to a *dimension* of *all* transference, which may fluctuate in the extent to which it occupies a position of figure or ground in the patient's experience of the analytic relationship. Kohut's work has illuminated the unique therapeutic importance of understanding and transforming those transference configurations in which the selfobject dimension is figure–in which, that is, the restoration or maintenance of self-organization is primary in motivating the patient's tie to the analyst. Even when this is not the case, however, and other dimensions of experience and human motivation–such as conflicts over loving, hating, desiring, and competing–emerge as most salient in structuring the transference, the selfobject dimension is never absent. So long as it is undisturbed, it operates silently in the background, enabling the patient to make contact with frightening and conflictual feelings.

An important implication of this conceptualization is that the analyst must continually assess the often subtly shifting figure-ground relationships among the selfobject and other dimensions of the transference that occur throughout the course of treatment. The assessment of what dimensions and psychological functions constitute figure and what constitute ground at any particular juncture of the analysis will directly determine the content and timing of transference interpretations (see Stolorow and Lachmann, 1980, 1981).

A second implication of this conceptualization is that the selfobject or developmental dimension of transference must be included in any effort to delineate the process of cure in psychoanalysis. We shall return to this issue later.

TRANSFERENCE AND THE THERAPEUTIC PROCESS

The Analyst's Contribution to the Transference

While a review of the voluminous literature on the role of the transference in the therapeutic relationship would take us beyond the intentions of this chapter, two broadly contrasting positions can be outlined. On one hand, transference has been understood as emanating entirely from the patient. The belief, implicit in the archeological model, that the patient makes a "false connection" or engages in "distortion" exemplifies this position. The analyst who adheres to this view will exercise care lest the transference become "contaminated." The recommendation that the analyst must avoid offering any gratification of the patient's infantile wishes will be strictly followed, so that these "frustrated" wishes can then emerge from repression and gain verbal expression. Abstinence is equated here with neutrality, on the assumption that the active frustration of the patient's wishes and needs constitutes a "neutral" act that neither colors the transference nor affects how these wishes and needs become manifest in the therapeutic relationship. Even Strachey's (1934) oft-quoted position that only transference interpetations are mutative is consistent with this viewpoint, because it implies that nontransference interpretations and other behaviors of the analyst will not alter the transference neurosis.

It is our view, by contrast, that any action, nonaction, or restrained action of the analyst can affect the transference on a variety of levels of psychological organization, according to its meanings for the patient. Furthermore, the analyst's attitudes and responses will influence which dimensions of the transference predominate at any given time. The relentlessly abstinent analyst, for example, who believes that the patient's infantile wishes must be exposed and renounced, will obstruct the developmental or selfobject dimension of the transference, and may in addition evoke intense conflicts over primitive hostility—an artifact of the therapeutic stance (Wolf, 1976). On the other hand, the analyst who strives actually to fulfill the patient's archaic needs may impede the development of more advanced modes of organization in the transference.

The contribution of the patient's transference to the production of the analyst's countertransference has found its place within psychoanalytic clinical theory. We are emphasizing here that the countertransference (broadly conceptualized as a manifestation of the analyst's psychological structures and organizing activity) has a decisive impact in shaping the transference and codetermining which of its specific dimensions will occupy the experiential foreground of the analysis. Transference and countertransference together form an intersubjective system of reciprocal mutual influence.

A second position, which arose in opposition to the view that transference is derived solely from the psychology of the patient, recommends that the analyst acknowledge his "actual" contribution to the transference. A typical example might involve a patient who reveals that he felt the analyst was angry with him during the prior session. An analyst who adheres to this second position might privately review the events of the previous session and determine for himself whether, indeed, he may have directly or indirectly conveyed annoyance to the patient. He might then acknowledge the "reality" of the patient's perception and then proceed to analyze the patient's reactions.

A disadvantage of the first position (that transference emanates entirely from the patient) is that it requires the patient to relinquish his organizing principles and psychic reality in favor of the analyst's. We object to the second view because, like the first, it places the analyst in the position of evaluating the veracity of the patient's perceptions, and the patient's experience is validated only because it coincides with that of the analyst. At its worst, this approach can tip the therapeutic balance in the direction of making the analyst's "reality" an explanation for the patient's reactions. The danger here lies in endowing the patient's perceptions with "truth" and "reality," not through the analytic process, but through the analyst's judgments.

Our own view is different from each of the two foregoing positions. When transference is conceptualized as organizing activity, it is assumed that the patient's experience of the therapeutic relationship is always shaped *both* by inputs from the analyst and by the structures of meaning into which these are assimilated by the patient. We would therefore do away with the rule of abstinence and its corresponding concept of neutrality and replace them with an attitude of sustained empathic inquiry, which seeks understanding of the patient's expressions from within the perspective of the patient's subjective frame of reference. From this vantage point, the reality of the patient's perceptions of the analyst is neither debated nor confirmed. Instead, these perceptions serve as points of departure for an exploration of the meanings and organizing principles that structure the patient's psychic reality.

This investigatory stance will itself have an impact on the transference. The patient's feeling of being understood, for example, can revive archaic oneness or merger experiences, which in turn may produce therapeutic effects (Silverman, Lachmann, and Milich, 1982). This brings us once again to the developmental dimension of the transference and its therapeutic action.

Transference Cures

An understanding of the developmental or selfobject dimension of the transference sheds new light on the role of transference in the process of psychoanalytic cure. Once established, the selfobject dimension of the transference is experienced to some degree by the patient as a "holding environment" (Winnicott, 1965), an archaic intersubjective context reinstating developmental processes of psychological differentiation and integration that were aborted and arrested during the patient's early formative years. Thus, when protected from protracted disruptions, the transference bond in and of itself can directly promote a process of psychological growth and structure formation. In our view, therefore, the singular importance of analyzing the patient's experiences of ruptures in the transference bond is found in the impact of such analysis in consistently mending the broken archaic tie and thereby permitting the arrested developmental process to resume once again.

We contend that it is the transference, especially in its developmental or selfobject dimension, that lends to interpretations their *mutative* power. Consider, for example, the transference context in which a traditional resistance analysis takes place. Experienced analysts know that clarifying the nature of a patient's resistance has no discernible therapeutic result unless the analyst is also able to identify the subjective danger or emotional conflict that makes the resistance a felt necessity. It is only when the analyst shows that he knows the patient's fear and anguish and thereby becomes established to some degree as a calming, containing selfobject—a *new* object separate and distinct from the dreaded parental imagoes—that conflictual regions of the patient's subjective life can emerge more freely.

The term *transference cure* has traditionally been applied pejoratively to indicate that a patient has "recovered" because of the unanalyzed influence of an unconscious instinctual tie to the analyst. What we are stressing here, in contrast, is the ubiquitous curative role played by the silent, at times unanalyzed selfobject dimension of the transference. We hold that every mutative therapeutic moment, even when based on interpretation of resistance and conflict, includes a significant element of selfobject transference cure.

Resolution of Transference

What is the ultimate fate of the transference in a successful psychoanalysis? Various authors have recommended that in the termination phase of an analysis the transference (especially the positive transference) must be resolved or dissolved through interpretation. Usually this means that the infantile wishes toward the analyst must be renounced.

The analytic relationship is a peculiar one in many respects. It is unique in being formed for a specific purpose—a therapeutic purpose for one of the participants. The requirement that it should end without residual transference feelings remaining seems to us to be unwarranted. Indeed, attempts to eliminate all traces of the transferences that have evolved in the course of analysis can adversely affect and even derail an otherwise successful treatment. Often it is believed that the transference must be dissolved for the sake of the patient's autonomy and that any residual transference feelings would constitute an infantilizing element, potentially undermining independence and object choices. In contrast, when transference is viewed as an expression of a universal human organizing tendency, analysis aims not for renunciation, but rather for the acceptance and integration of the transference experience into the fabric of the patient's analytically expanded psychological organization. The transference, thus integrated, greatly enriches the patient's affective life and contributes a repertoire of therapeutically achieved developmental attainments.

With regard to so-called infantile wishes, needs, and fantasies, it has never been adequately demonstrated that they can or should be renounced. Within an expanded and more evolved psychological organization, they can be welcomed, just as any valued possession can find a place on the mantelpiece, to be used on special occasions. The remaining love and hate for the analyst, including their archaic roots, can thus be acknowledged and accepted, without their having either to be requited or negated, or presumed to constitute an interference with the patient's current living. Ordinarily, after treatment has ended, the residual analytic transference will gradually recede from its preeminent position, relatively central in the patient's psychological world, to a position where it serves as a bridge to a more complex, differentiated, and richly experienced life.

CONCLUSION

Transference in its essence refers neither to regression, displacement, projection, nor distortion, but rather to the assimilation of the analytic relationship into the thematic structures of the patient's personal subjective world. Thus conceived, transference is an expression of the universal psychological striving to organize experience and create meanings. This broad conceptualization of transference holds numerous advantages over earlier ones. It can encompass the multiple dimensions of transference, including especially its developmental dimension, and it sheds light on the relationship of transference to resistance. It clarifies the contributions of both analyst and patient in shaping the patient's experience of the therapeutic relationship. It illuminates the role of the transference in the process of psychoanalytic cure and in the patient's life after analysis is completed. Most important of all, the concept of transference as organizing activity, by encouraging an unwavering inquiry into the patient's subjective frame of reference, opens a clear and unobstructed window to the patient's psychological world, and to its expansion, evolution, and enrichment.

4

Bonds That Shackle, Ties That Free

Margaret Mahler's pioneering work highlighted the central developmental importance of the process of self-differentiation—the evolving sense of oneself as a demarcated and distinctive human being with a unique affective life and an individualized array of personal values and aims. She observed that this process "reverberates throughout the life cycle. It is never finished; it remains always active; new phases of the life cycle see new derivatives of the earliest processes still at work" (Mahler, Pine, and Bergman, 1975, p. 3). Although, in her formal developmental scheme, the phase of separation-individuation begins at the age of four to five months, arising out of the matrix of an undifferentiated "symbiotic phase," passages in her work point to the presence of self-differentiation processes at birth (see also Stern, 1985). Mahler's observations support the view that a tenacious striving for self-delineation powerfully organizes the developmental process throughout its course.

Mahler also identified the specific affective states that color the self-differentiation process, as well as those that result from its derailment. The dominant mood accompanying self-differentiation was one of unmistakable elation, manifesting itself

> in a quasi-delusional but age-adequate sense of grandeur, omnipotence, and conquest. This mood of the junior toddler—at the crest of mastery of many of his autonomous functions, the paradigm of which is locomotion—necessarily had to give way to a more realistic appraisal of his smallness in relation to the outside world [Mahler et al., 1975, p. 213].

The infant's experience of relative helplessness punctures his "inflated sense of omnipotence," forcing him to recognize that he is small and powerless and that he has to cope with overwhelming odds because of his separateness. Thus, the dominant mood shifts to one of soberness and even temporary depression. From these observations it can be concluded that elation is dominant when self-differentiation processes are engaged, whereas depression is preeminent when these processes are obstructed.

Kohut's (1984) formulation of the role of selfobject functions in the developmental process led him to a view of psychological development that was distinctly different from Mahler's. Specifically, he objected to the postulation of separation as the supreme goal of development and regarded it instead as an indication of developmental failure. As an alternative, he proposed a lifelong need for selfobject experiences and a developmental line of continuing, maturationally transformed selfobject relations:

> Self psychology holds that self-selfobject relationships form the essence of psychological life from birth to death, that a move from dependence (symbiosis) to independence (autonomy) in the psychological sphere is no more possible, let alone desirable, than a corresponding move from a life dependent on oxygen to a life independent of it in the biological sphere. The developments that characterize normal psychological life must, in our view, be seen in the changing nature of the relationship between the self and its selfobjects, but not in the self's relinquishment of selfobjects [p. 47].

In this chapter we offer a resolution of the apparent theoretical antithesis between separation-individuation theory and the concept of changing selfobject relationships throughout life, by stressing that specific, maturationally evolving selfobject experiences are absolutely necessary for facilitating, consolidating, expanding, and sustaining the development of individualized selfhood during the entire life cycle. This developmental progression becomes disrupted when the requisite selfobject experiences are absent or unsteady. We are contending that the process of self-differentiation, as well as its derailments, always occurs within a specific intersubjective system or context.

A key question of current psychoanalytic interest concerns the relationship between developmental failure and the formation of psychic conflict. Mahler recognized the importance of the mother in "shaping, promoting, or hindering the individual child's . . . development" (Mahler et al., 1975, p. 202), and she specified the contribution of the mother's personality structure, her parental functioning, and, especially, her unconscious expectations of her child. However, in discussing the *conflicts* that accompany the self-differentiation process, Mahler tended to conceptualize them in exclusively intrapsychic terms:

> Here is the conflict: On the one hand is the toddler's feeling of helplessness in his realization of separateness, and on the other hand is his valiant defense of what he cherishes as the emerging autonomy of his body. In this struggle for individuation, and the concomitant anger about his helplessness, the toddler tries to reinflate his sense of self, to approximate the forever lost illusion of omnipotence . . . [p. 222].

The conflict that we believe to be central to the process of self-differentiation and to the emergence of individualized selfhood is not the one described by Mahler. A toddler's protracted feeling of helplessness in the experience of separateness would, to us, indicate a failure in essential caregiving functions. These necessarily include not only resonance with and sharing of the child's buoyant enthusiasm and pleasure in the emergence of his own particularity, but also attunement to and containment of his disappointment in his limitations and failings, coupled with a sustaining confidence in his growing abilities and ultimate success. When such resonance and attuned responsiveness accompany the various facets of the child's differentiating processes, unbridled expansiveness will gradually be modulated and a sense of confident efficacy in the vigorous pursuit of individualized goals will be acquired. Once the attunement of the caregiving system has resulted in a stable and positively toned sense of self, limitations that the child inevitably experiences in himself and in the surround are generally not seriously threatening. Under these circumstances, experiences of limitation may actually mobilize the child's determination, resourcefulness, and creativity. When the requisite selfobject experiences are absent, by contrast, the child's sense of self will oscillate between sequestered grandiose fantasies and painful feelings of smallness and depletion, which necessitate the lonely efforts at restorative inflation so accurately described by Mahler. This latter child is recognizable in the adult patient whose sense of self remains threatened by any limitation or setback and who therefore must repeatedly close down channels of interest and opportunity in order to avert tormenting descents into preoccupations with what he is not or cannot do.

Mahler's explanations of obstructions to the process of self-differentiation often placed primary emphasis on the conflictual aggression that awareness of separation was presumed inevitably to mobilize:

> Throughout the whole course of separation-individuation, one of the most important developmental tasks of the evolving ego is that of coping with the aggressive drive in the face of the gradually increasing awareness of separateness. The success with which this is achieved depends on the strength of the primitive ego . . . [p. 226].

Such accounts leave out the specific intersubjective contexts in which the experiences are taking place—exuberant distinctiveness, for example, occurring as an emerging and shared experience within an intact selfobject tie, as opposed to lonely and isolated separation when the child's vigorous assertion of his own perceptions precipitates an experience of loss of a vitally needed bond. The trajectory of individualized selfhood encompasses differentiated perceptual, affective, and cognitive spheres of experience and includes such developmental accomplishments as self and object boundary delineation, intentionality and the sense of personal agency, and a continuity of purposeful movement toward the achievement of goals of increasing particularity. A primary source of conflict is the clashing of emergent affect states, rooted in developmentally imperative self-differentiation processes, with equally imperative needs to maintain vital ties inimical to such differentiation.

When patients whose strivings for differentiated selfhood have been aborted enter analysis, they seek a safe milieu in which the conflicts that have obstructed, derailed, or compromised their development can emerge. An indispensable feature of such an environment is the analyst's commitment to a stance of sustained empathic inquiry. Especially important are the understandings to be attained from the close observation of the patient's perception of the analyst and of the analyst's impact on the patient's sense of self—of how the evolving tie to the analyst is experienced as freeing, or further shackling, the patient's strivings for self-delineation. Such inquiry enables the patient to form a therapeutic bond in which gradual access can be gained to those regions of his self-experience that have been repressed and disavowed, sequestered in their archaic forms.

The reinstatement of aborted differentiating processes may be signaled in many ways and take a wide variety of forms; for example, a change in appearance or a tentative musing about a new interest or discovery. Commonly, such reinstatements occur in a form that makes the analyst's understanding of and approach to the problem of resistance crucial. In an especially pertinent passage, Kohut (1984) wrote:

> Defense motivation in analysis will be understood in terms of activities undertaken in the service of *psychological survival*, that is, as the patient's attempt to save at least that sector of his nuclear self, however small and precariously established it may be, that he has been able to construct and maintain despite serious insufficiencies in the development-enhancing matrix of the selfobjects of childhood [p. 115, emphasis added].

This conception of resistance is invaluable in the analysis of conflicts over self-differentiation as these become engaged in the analytic transference, for it is often in the manifestations of the patient's "resistance" that we find the clearest evidence of the thwarted strivings for self-demarcation, now reactivated in the analytic situation. Once such resistances are recognized not as malignant opposition to the analytic process, but as efforts by the patient to protect the organization of his self-experience from encroachment and usurpation, then it becomes critical to explore as fully as possible how, from the patient's perspective, the analyst has come to embody such a threat to the patient's essential selfhood. That information can become available only to the extent of the patient's belief in the analyst's readiness to receive it.

Among the most noxious of early pathogenic situations are those in which a child's attempts to communicate an experience of being psychologically injured or undermined by a caregiver result in a prolonged disruption of the vitally needed tie. When the child consistently is unable to communicate such experiences without perceiving that he is damaging or unwelcome to the caregiver, a watershed in the relationship occurs whereby a painful inner confict becomes structuralized. It is this pathogenic process that is repeated in analysis when critical information concerning the impact of the analyst on the patient is interpreted as reflecting malignant intrapsychic mechanisms within the patient, such as splitting, projection, or aggressive devaluation. Such ideas generally occur to an analyst when his own feeling of well-being is threatened by the patient's expressions, and interpretations of resistance under these circumstances serve primarily to reconstitute the analyst's own sense of self. Such reactions, if uncorrected, weld more tightly the shackles that the patient is attempting to throw off. It is at such points of potential stalemate that dedication to a stance of sustained empathic inquiry produces the greatest yields, by inviting detailed investigation of the elements in the analyst's activity to which the patient has been selectively responding, and of which the analyst may have been unaware. Exploration of the specific *meanings* that the analyst's activities have for the patient, together with reconstructions of how these meanings were acquired developmentally, then become possible. It is the full and continuing articulation of the patient's affective experience of the analyst that establishes an intersubjective context in which the arrested process of self-differentiation can become reinstated.

We contend that derailment of the self-differentiation process occurs in an intersubjective situation in which central affect states associated with the development of individualized selfhood are consistently not responded to or are actively rejected. A fundamental psychic conflict thereby becomes enduringly established between the requirement that one's developmental course must conform to the emotional needs of caregivers and the inner imperative that its evolution be firmly rooted in a vitalizing affective core of one's own. Several outcomes of this basic conflict are possible. One is a life of relentless, tormenting ambivalence, endlessly torn between inner aspirations and needed relationships that seem irreconcilably opposed. This is the path of wrenching indecision and noncommitment. Or the child may attempt to preserve and protect his core of individualized vitality at the expense of object ties by adopting a pattern of resolute defiance and rebellion. This is the path of isolation and estrangement. Alternatively, the child may abandon or severely compromise central affective strivings in order to maintain indispensable ties. This is the path of submission and chronic depression.

In an earlier contribution (Brandchaft, 1986), clinical material was provided illustrating the developmental origins of a pattern of submission and depression—the bond that shackles. The nature of the evolving transference experience that eventually brought about a liberating realignment was also discussed. We now present an illustration of the derailments that can occur when a different pathway, that of rebellion, is chosen in order to safeguard a precariously differentiated self.

CLINICAL ILLUSTRATION

Martin is an engaging and handsome young man who made several previous attempts at psychoanalysis. He entered the present treatment with a number of complaints, including a virulent hypochondriasis, a diffuse vulnerability, a tendency to violent rage, and a marital and interpersonal life marked by discontent and strife. Although he was dedicated to his work and to his children, he experienced very little pleasure from life, and his difficulty establishing limits for himself left him chronically exhausted.

Soon after the treatment had begun, a striking pattern of behavior emerged that signaled the engagement of archaic differentiating processes within the transference. Martin began regularly to come late for his sessions. The lateness would vary from about 10 minutes to 30 or more. Not infrequently he would miss sessions altogether. Sometimes he would call to cancel; at other times he would not. He also began running later and later in the payment of fees. For some time, any attempt to investigate this behavior might bring about the payment but would also evoke a response clearly indicating that it was imperative for the analyst to recognize that Martin could not be compelled or coerced to do anything to please the analyst or fulfill any of the analyst's needs. If the analyst communicated any expectations of Martin, this automatically provoked an intense negative reaction. Martin invariably responded by distancing himself and by resorting to enactments that reinforced boundaries he experienced as under threat. The lateness and missed sessions, the latter in strings of as many as six weeks, continued for several years.

Early in the analysis, Martin also began to experience the emergence of intense, archaic selfobject needs. These were frequently presented in a demanding and aggressive form that seemed overwhelming to the analyst, and when the analyst failed to meet them, Martin reacted with intense disappointment. For example, on one occasion after Martin had failed to appear for the first 35 minutes of the session, the analyst left the office and returned to find him furious at being kept waiting. Martin had felt a physical reaction to the door between the waiting room and consultation room being shut. It was later learned that when he was a child he had been besieged by unimaginable terrors when put to bed alone in his room. He would make his way into his parents' bedroom, urgently wanting to be comforted. However, they apparently felt intruded on and attributed his behavior to an inordinate need for attention, which they were afraid would result in his forever having to have his own way. So they locked their door and in this way attempted to cure him.

On another occasion in the analysis, Martin entered through an open door some 15 or 20 minutes late and found the analyst answering a telephone call. He was outraged that the time he felt belonged to him had been given to someone else without his having been consulted, and he insisted that the justice of his position be acknowledged. Later, the significance of this demand as a precondition for the establishment of a continuing bond would become more understandable. It then emerged that the early context from within which Martin's passionate arbitrariness had crystallized was one in which his caregivers believed, and required him to believe, that everything of value that Martin possessed came from them, to be given, taken away, or redistributed as they saw fit. In reaction against this requirement, Martin chose a course of chronic rebellion.

The most difficult problems posed for the analyst involved sorting out his own reactions and their impact on Martin. This was especially exacting because Martin had developed an unusual acuity of perception, especially for dissonant, unattuned, or misattuned responses, and a directness and intensity of expression that were equally unusual. These characteristics were particularly dominant during the early phase of the analysis, as Martin was extremely vigilant and guarded in order to protect himself against the primary threat that increasing engagement posed for him. He was firmly convinced that the price of a harmonious tie to the analyst would be submission to the analyst, a betrayal of his trust by the analyst, and abandonment of his own strivings for individualized selfhood. It was threats such as these that had compelled him to limit, control, or withdraw from every previous relationship. This solution had left him feeling alienated and alone, endowing every achievement with an unbearable hollowness and every victory with a growing sense of empty isolation.

A crucial episode contributed importantly to the analyst's understanding of his own reactions and to his ability to decenter from these in order increasingly to attune himself to Martin's experiences. One day Martin sauntered into the session, unusually late, having spent much of the last session deploring some insensitivity and lack of consideration on the part of the analyst. Such diatribes had often elicited a genuine feeling of admiration in the analyst for the unerring and flawless quality of Martin's perceptions and for his forthright expression. On this particular day, however, the analyst felt irritated and put upon by Martin's complaints of the previous day and by his lateness. Before the patient could begin speaking, the analyst asked him if he was not aware of any lack of consideration in keeping the analyst waiting so consistently, when he, Martin, so much hated to be in that position himself. Martin sat upright, looked squarely at the analyst, and said calmly:

> Listen. If you are asking if I am upset about being late, the answer is yes. And if you are pissed off with me, tell me so and don't pretend what you are doing is part of the analysis. I have lived all my life with people being pissed off with me, and then saying they are not and always that it is for my own good! What I don't understand and don't like in you is not that you are upset but your subterfuge. You can insist that I have to come on time in order to keep you from getting out of joint and I will try to do it. If I can't, as I expect, then I will quit. But whether I came on time or whether I didn't, make no mistake about it, nothing fundamental about me would change!

Behind Martin's incessant and escalating demands the analyst gradually came to recognize a well of unfulfilled yearnings. These did not necessarily have to be satisfied, but it was critical that they be responded to with acceptance, respect, and an effort to understand them, however provocatively they were expressed. Martin had a volcanic, thundering rage—the result of repeatedly exposing his needs, especially his needs to have *his* experience understood, to impenetrable caregivers. He massively repudiated his longings for connection with others, in consequence of his automatic anticipation that conflict and submission would be their inexorable outcome. It was this anticipation that continued to shape the intensity and direction of his wishes and his reactions.

Until Martin could experience the analyst as accepting his lateness or absences, this behavior could not be analyzed. Martin was exquisitely attuned to any irritation, harshness, or dissatisfaction with him and to any attempt to seduce or compel him to fit in with the analyst's psychological or practical requirements. To any such misattunement to Martin's subjective state and to the legitimacy of his underlying motivation, Martin reacted with rage or with an intensification of his staying-away behavior, sometimes accompanied by other enactments designed to restore a sense of distinctness. Martin's sensitivity to the quality of the analyst's affect as opposed to the content of the analyst's words was particularly striking. The interventions that Martin experienced as most noxious were those in which he sensed defensiveness on the analyst's part or any attempt to repudiate Martin's perceptions of the analyst's out-of-tune state. In such instances, florid symptoms would emerge that concretized the patient's experience of the assault on his sense of self. These included severe hypochondriacal anxiety and paranoidlike fears of thugs, burglars, and other environmental dangers.

The analyst was able to decenter from his own reactions to Martin's lateness and absences through his growing understanding of the developmental process the patient was attempting to revive and of his own indispensable role in that process. Specifically, the analyst had to accept Martin's sense that it was essential to reinforce self-boundaries by staying away when he felt them threatened, rather than to attend for fear that the analyst would be displeased with him and throw him out. The meanings of Martin's lateness could then emerge, and change could come about through genuine transformational processes, rather than compliance.

Similar enactments are frequently regarded by analysts as "acting out," supposedly arising from fears of commitment to the analytic process, hostility toward and depreciation of the analyst, pathological entitlement attitudes, and a variety of other reactions deriving from projections of or displacements from archaic parental imagoes. Such interpretations are apt to occur to the analyst when the patient's behavior constitutes a threat to his own sense of self. Under such pressures, the analyst is inclined to wish to put a stop to the behavior, which, when not understood from within the patient's perspective, is mistakenly regarded as being detrimental to the patient and to the analytic process. All such responses from the analyst are likely to be experienced by the patient as part of a bond that shackles, because they superimpose an alien and extrinsic organization of experience onto his own, thereby derailing the self-differentiating process and depriving it of a sustaining matrix.

We wish to emphasize a finding that became unmistakable as the analysis progressed. Even in those instances in which Martin's lateness could definitely be linked to some experience of misattunement in the preceding session, it was neither the earlier asynchrony nor the lateness, nor any other reaction on Martin's part, that resulted in serious disjunction. Rather, it was invariably a *subsequent* failure by the analyst to connect empathically with Martin's dysphoric state of mind, and to appreciate the impact of the prior misattunement on Martin's sense of self and hopes for himself, that would lead to a marked increase in his guardedness and avoidance behavior and to a feeling of unending despair.

Careful focus on the intersubjective context in which Martin's lateness was occurring made possible a deeper understanding of its meanings. One aspect concerned Martin's state of mind as he attempted to get up to attend his session each morning. His alarm clock would ring, but he could not respond. He described his mind as a clouded, inchoate, unorganizable haze that he could not shake clear. His eyelids were lead weights. Sometimes he would drag himself to the shower and turn hot and cold water on himself at full volume, but he felt no sense of coherence, no connection to goals, and especially no sense of the passage of time. What he thought was five minutes could turn out to be thirty. The first thoughts that formed were automatic and familiar. Once more he had "fucked up!" Once more he was going to be late! The analyst then materialized in his thoughts as yet another person he had disappointed. The analyst, in his stoical way, might say nothing, but Martin would be able to detect, in the unsmiling and stereotyped greeting, in the weariness, arched eyebrow, and turned down corner of the mouth, a dreary resignation at having him as a patient. It became clear that although Martin's initial motivation was to get to his sessions on time, he was unable, without analytic understanding, to sustain that goal. What interfered was the erosive impact on his sense of self of the particular difficulties he kept encountering, as well as his perception that the analyst's confidence in him was being similarly eroded by his failures. The devastating impact of any limitation, setback, or failure on Martin's basic definition of himself was emerging as a primary area of developmental derailment that had shaped the course his life had taken.

As a child, Martin had experienced severe problems in getting out of bed and readying himself for school. He had to be constantly prodded by his parents, and the more they prodded and chastised, the more he clung to the pillow, which made no demands on him and which he could mold to his needs. Martin's parents had chosen him, their first-born son, to bring honor and glory to the family. He was to endow it with the recognition and admiration they themselves had failed to elicit. Thus, they found their son's aberrant behavior utterly incomprehensible and frightening. They could not understand how he could possibly be afraid of going to bed or of going to school, or of the teasing and cruelty of other children, which so terrified him. Fear and aversion to school in the young hero-to-be was for them an "excuse" for his weakness and an unmitigated humiliation and symbol of their failure. When his behavior persisted, they would call him a boy made of mush, never to amount to anything, a child who brought dishonor to his father, a man who worked so hard without a murmur of complaint and got up each morning raring to go! Martin's parents believed that if he would only go to bed on time and eat the right foods, he would have no trouble getting up in the morning. They could not understand his wish to stay up a little longer before facing the terrors of being alone and feeling banished. They did not understand that, for Martin, being alone was not merely being alone. It was being alone with the reflection of himself acquired throughout the day and reinforced just before he entered his room—alone with all the bad things he was and had said and done, and with all the good things he had failed to do and be. His parents could not understand that the threat posed by their relentless disparagement of him became concretized in agonizing fears of boogey men, kidnappers, and terrifying apparitions. Instead, they wistfully told stories of how little Martin, at one year of age, had lifted himself above the crib bars, climbed out of bed, and sat at the head of the stairs, and of how they added two feet to the height of the crib to keep him in.

A second feature of Martin's lateness surfaced. It was one that pervaded his entire existence—the absolute necessity of controlling his own world and his own course. His need not to give in to someone else's wishes had become hypertrophied as his only means of establishing and maintaining his self-boundaries against constant erosion and violation.

Martin's mother emerged in his memories as a beautiful woman who had never wanted to marry and who, before she quite knew what had happened, found herself with four squalling, quarrelling, clamoring boys assailing her. Martin remembered her as a brooding, lurking presence, always trying desperately to train them so as to unburden herself and gain some relief. She tried unsuccessfully to toilet train Martin when he was eight months old, because urine and feces represented everything odious, disgusting, and enslaving about him to her. She tried again when he was two, but again with no success. He early became a chronic irritant, a constant reminder to her of her failures and of her own bondage; and she became the same to him—a nagging, screaming, fusilade of "don'ts," "why can'ts," "can't you evers," and "when will yous" that often began the moment he came into her presence.

Martin's mother seemed to him to live at the junction between weariness and icy withdrawal on one side and reproachfulness on the other. Most upsetting was her utter unpredictability. He could never know at what moment she would interrupt a conversation with him to slap him in the face because he was fidgeting too much, or reach into the back seat of the car and whack him because he was making too much noise. His childhood, Martin recalled, was like waiting for a Nazi siren to go off. Yet occasionally his mother would flash a smile, her eyes emit a glint or a gleam, when he did something that really pleased her. He could, without protest, put on the clothes she had picked out for him and thereby show he cared about her and not about the boys at school, who would tease and humiliate him. He didn't have to make such a fuss about the chafing that the Brooks Brothers trousers would inflict on his wool-sensitive legs. He remembered that she would beam with pride when, hoping to evoke through him the glow she had never been able to extract for herself, she cleaned, polished, and dressed him in the uniform for his weekly parade before her parents. "Everything about this boy is beautiful," his mother would then say, "I just want to eat him up."

One other experience brought heavenly serenity, that smile of pleasure to Martin's mother's eyes. She loved jewelry, fine furs, and silverware; these made the difference between feeling cherished or deprived. The only consistently intense interest that he had ever observed in her was shopping. That made her come alive and brought a glow to her face, except when he spoiled it by being a pest about waiting when she took him with her. He would come home with her from shopping and watch as, magically transformed, she paraded her day's treasures and recited her accomplishments before his father.

The grandiosity and expansiveness fostered by his mother's showing him off came to serve important defensive and restitutive functions for Martin. Sometimes he would go to his room and there, in his own, protected space, dream the dreams of glory that enabled him to repair a battered and undermined sense of himself. These dreams would materialize a world in which he could do anything, make millions, be acclaimed, and then triumphantly appear before his parents to show how wrong they had been in telling him so many times that he would be a nothing. He imagined laying his treasures at his mother's feet, wiping away her black moods and sullen withdrawals. Once and for all he would reclaim his heritage by restoring her world, which—he was forever being told with a thousand cues, raised eyebrows, and turned down corners of a mouth—had collapsed because of something he had done or failed to do.

Martin acquired several lasting characteristics from his relationship with his mother, which also came to structure his experience of the analyst. He learned to stay away as the only certain means of protection. He developed and retained a burning ambition to become as rich as Croesus so that he would never again be helpless to produce the glow of admiration for which he continued to yearn. At the same time, he showed stubborn opposition to paying for anything, including his treatment. Every bill from the analyst was an excruciatingly painful reminder of the limits of the relationship and therefore of his own limitations. For Martin, the analyst's fee seemed to confirm a principle that had come to dominate his inner life—that every relationship was contingent on his performing and that he *had* to pay in order to be liked. Thus, to pay was unbearably degrading to him, and so he devised myriad ways to drag his heels, to postpone payments, to pay in driblets, to pay and not to pay in the same act.

Perhaps the most damaging consequence of Martin's early relationship with his mother was a severe developmental arrest in the area of self-differentiation. He could not, on his own, maintain any positive self-definition, and his sense of himself had come to be entirely dependent on the availability of admiring and responsive women in his environment. Correspondingly, he remained extremely vulnerable to alterations in the mood of partners he had chosen, which could produce devastating collapses in his self-esteem. This extreme vulnerability had already begun to have an overriding effect during his childhood. When he had been put to bed and was alone, he could not counteract the pictures of himself as bad, selfish, or defective that would begin to overwhelm him. It was that intersubjectively induced view of himself that lay behind the night terrors for which he had sought to be comforted by his parents. This feature of his self-experience emerged in the analysis when Martin disclosed the tormenting self-reproaches that accompanied any failure or disappointment and that underlay a persistent and severe insomnia.

From the unsatisfactory alternatives presented to Martin in his relationship with his mother—bondage or isolation—the young boy turned to his father, an earnest, hard-working man. His father was unusual in many ways, and they had a special relationship. He was frequently a source of comfort for Martin, particularly when Martin looked up to him and asked for advice. But his father could also suddenly and unpredictably change. He could not bear to see anything going wrong without attempting to fix it, and for much of what went wrong he found Martin to be the cause. He especially blamed Martin for his mother's bad days. "What's the matter with you," his father would say, "How come you don't listen to your mother? I slept in a cellar with rats and I loved my mother, and your mother keeps such a nice house, slaves for you, and you don't appreciate anything." If his brother and he had a fight, Martin was the older and therefore responsible. If he had a stomach ache, it was because he had eaten "all that crap." Every deviation established anew that Martin was not a member of the clan—his hair, his disrespect, his willfulness, his fearfulness, and his proneness to illness. Martin needed to do things his own way, and his father regarded him as a threat to his power and to his own peace of mind. Mostly his father attempted to control Martin with withering sarcasm and continuous teasing. Sometimes it went further, and Martin was often threatened with being cast out—to an orphanage or to military school. Once Martin's older cousin had been caught taking drugs. "If I ever catch any of you becoming an addict," his father threatened, "I swear to God I will feed you a poisoned meatball. And if they catch me and send me to the electric chair, I will die a happy man because I will have cleansed my conscience by ridding the world of a scourge I brought into it."

Even after a stable transference tie had become established, the missing of sessions continued. For a time, if there was an unusually productive session, Martin was even more apt to miss the following session than if it had gone poorly. He continued even more urgently to need the time and space, to counteract the increasing threat to his boundaries that the greater engagement posed. As he became more secure, he felt the analyst's displeasure acutely whenever he would depart from the code he was convinced the analyst expected him to follow. He must stop his "acting out," be understanding to his wife, take care of his children, and lead a "clean life."

One day he appeared at the office quite late. He spoke about his lateness, saying that he had risen at 6 a.m. and could have taken a shower and come on time. But he was tired. He recounted a number of incidents during the previous day that he had come to recognize as having an enfeebling effect on his sense of himself. Following such experiences, it was always hard for him to get out of bed the next day. It was a chore, and he had to concentrate to do it. He experienced a constant battle with exhaustion. With the analyst, he went on, he was recreating his early childhood. His ambitions had been tied to the expectations of his father and they always exceeded his abilities. He was a constant disappointment to his parents.

> When I take a day off, I lie around in bed. I read. I lunch at my leisure and then I go to a bookstore. I want to lie in my crib and not be expected to perform. In the morning I am in a dreamlike state in which I am recovering from the demands that have dehumanized and exhausted me. If I don't sleep well, it has a terrible effect on me. I was never permitted to lie in bed. "Why are you always tired?" my father would ask. I was always exhausted and I always got the impression that there was something intrinsically not right. Always I was pushed by external regulation—to go to

> school on time, to wear the clothes they wanted me to wear. I wanted to control my environment, but my mother and father kept pushing me.
>
> My lateness is a present-day manifestation of having been constantly invaded and usurped, of having my space violated. Lateness is the last stall; it is a desperate measure that comes from being put on a schedule that is not my own, being sold on it and having to abide by it in order to exist. The real reason is that I have lacked an environment in which there is a sense of protection of my own time and my own space. If I objected seriously to my mother's and father's infiltration, I could be thrown out, sent to an orphanage, or later to military school.
>
> Lateness is my inability to embrace the day ahead because I have been sold into conscription. Each day only holds an endless series of engagements, each of which is marked by what I *should* do. I have adopted this life form in order to survive. But then survival itself has become of dubious value.

As the analysis continued, it was marked by periods of regular attendance, punctuated by other periods in which for five or six weeks Martin would stay away. Nonetheless, many significant changes were occurring. One was the reappearance of a gentleness and caring, which had been all but crushed by his wall of defensiveness. An interest in artistic and poetic expression also took form and began to produce a feeling of peaceful pleasure within him. Martin slowly became able to accept limitations in himself and in others. Succeeding sessions clarified what the stance taken by the analyst had meant to Martin. In the fifth year of the analysis, after suffering a serious financial setback, Martin withdrew from treatment and missed about 25 sessions. The following is the note the analyst recorded after Martin had returned:

> Martin returned this week after an absence of six weeks. There were two sessions in which he told something about what had kept him away, then one session missed, and then he returned again. He began by saying that he wanted me to know how important it was for him to be able to come back after he had stayed away and to be greeted with a smile and a gesture of warmth. He said that all the times when he had been welcomed back without

> being made to feel bad about not having been here had had an irradicable effect. Those experiences had catapulted him over a jungle of thickets and had enabled him to begin to feel whole and hopeful. And he wanted me to know that these interruptions reflected not a limitation of the treatment but, as he increasingly recognizes, its expansion; and a limitation in a self that is healing and also expanding.

In the sessions that followed, Martin was able to articulate and reflect upon the feelings of apprehension that automatically accompanied the development of a stronger tie to the analyst. "For me," he said, "this tie to you is like a biopsy I keep sending to the lab to see whether a cancer has yet appeared."

While distancing and rebellious behavior had characterized Martin's attempts to differentiate himself from the analyst, threats to such self-differentiation had been pervasive in Martin's experience of the transference bond. He was afraid that his critical perceptions of and affective reactions to the analyst would create an unbridgeable separation, as we have described. Similar fears extended to his choices of companions, to his sources of pleasure and aesthetic interests, and to the goals and ideals that he had come to embrace. He was always scanning the face and posture of the analyst for signs of uneasiness or disapproval whenever he reported an act or idea that he felt diverged from what the analyst expected of him. He was convinced that the analyst would feel damaged or disaffected by the success for which Martin yearned and of which he felt he was capable. Searching the analyst's face, he said one day:

> I know I ought to trust you, but I don't, and now I feel like running out of here. I feel like I'm up against a stone wall and I shouldn't go on. "Why do you want to hurt this man?" I ask myself. "He's been so good to you, here all the time, made it easier when you had trouble paying the bill, helps cure you of your hypochondria. What do you want of him?" I need encouragement to continue, but either we are going to get this out in the open once and for all, or it will just get covered over and over again.
>
> I don't believe you. I don't believe you will help me do what *I* want to do. I don't believe that when I lose weight and become trim and handsome you won't think about your own youth and your

> not being a good athlete. I don't believe that when I'm with a beautiful lady you won't be sad that it's not you with her; that if I have ten million dollars and work three days a week you won't be eating yourself up with disappointment with what you do. I know this because I see you sometimes tired and depressed.

Through such forthright communications it became possible to bring out into the open the different facets of the development of Martin's selfhood that had been interrupted and become intensely conflictual. It also became possible to illuminate the underlying conflict in all its ubiquity—the conviction pervading every developmental level that resonant responsiveness could be elicited from his environment only at the price of alienation from the affective core of his own essential self. Increasingly, the analytic work became centered on investigating the experiences with the analyst that kept this conviction alive and on unearthing the encoded developmental contexts that had imparted to this nodal organizing principle its invariant and heretofore unchallengeable character.

CONCLUSION

Specific, maturationally evolving selfobject experiences are required for sustaining the development of individualized selfhood throughout life. Pathogenic derailments of this developmental process occur in intersubjective situations in which the central affect states that accompany self-differentiation are consistently not responded to or are actively rejected. A fundamental inner conflict thereby becomes established between the requirement that self-development must mold to the needs of caregivers and the imperative that it take root from a vitalizing affective core of one's own. Patients enter analysis with hopes for an intersubjective context in which thwarted strivings for differentiated selfhood may become liberated (the tie that frees) and with fears that the violations of self-experience encountered in childhood will be repeated with the analyst (the bond that shackles). As seen in our clinical illustration, resistances in such cases encapsulate the patient's truncated efforts at self-delineation, and it is crucial for the progress of the analysis and for the patient's development to investigate in detail all the ways in which the patient experiences the analyst as a threat to his essential selfhood.

5

Affects and Selfobjects

(written in collaboration with Daphne Socarides Stolorow)

We stated in chapter 2 that we regard the concept of selfobject function to be one of three foundational pillars of Kohut's psychoanalytic psychology of the self. However, we perceive this concept to be vulnerable to two maladies that can afflict important theoretical ideas in the early phases of their evolution. On one hand, there is a tendency for the concept to remain unduly static and narrow, restricted to the particular idealizing and mirroring ties delineated by its originator. On the other hand, in the enthusiasm of theoretical expansion, there is the danger of the concept becoming overly general and imprecise, as when it is extended to encompass almost any caregiving activity that a child or developmentally arrested adult may require. Our intention in the present chapter is to offer an expansion and refinement of the selfobject concept that we believe can skirt both the Scylla of theoretical encrustation and the Charybdis of overgeneralization. It is our contention that selfobject functions pertain fundamentally to the integration of *affect* into the organization of self-experience, and that the need for selfobject ties pertains most centrally to the need for attuned responsiveness to affect states in all stages of the life cycle. To develop this claim we must first examine briefly the pivotal role of affect and affect integration in the structuralization of the self.

As we indicated in chapter 2, we conceive of the self as an *organization of experience*, referring specifically to the structure of a person's experience of himself. The self, from this vantage point, is a psychological structure through which self-experience acquires cohesion and continuity, and by virtue of which self-experience assumes its characteristic shape and enduring organization. The fundamental role of affectivity in the organization of self-experience has been alluded to by generations of analytic investigators and has found considerable confirmation in recent studies of the patterning of early infant-caregiver interactions (Emde, 1983; Lichtenberg, 1983; Basch, 1985; Stern, 1985; Beebe, 1986; Demos, 1987). Stern (1985) regards affectivity as a "self-invariant," contributing, during the first months of life, to the development of "the sense of a core self" (p. 69). He argues that "interaffectivity"—the mutual sharing of affective states—is "the most pervasive and clinically germaine feature of intersubjective relatedness" (p. 138), determining for the infant "the shape of and extent of the shareable inner universe" (p. 152). Drawing on the work of Sander (1982), Demos (1987) claims that the rudiments of the infant's sense of self crystallize around its inner experience of recurrent affect states, and she points to the critical part played by the responsiveness of the caregiving environment in fostering the development of the infant's affect- (and self-) regulatory capacities. These studies bring into clear view the central importance of affect integration in the evolution and consolidation of self-experience, as well as the intersubjective matrix in which this developmental process takes place.

Affects can be seen as organizers of self-experience throughout development, if met with the requisite affirming, accepting, differentiating, synthesizing, and containing responses from caregivers. An absence of steady, attuned responsiveness to the child's affect states leads to minute but significant derailments of optimal affect integration and to a propensity to dissociate or disavow affective reactions because they threaten the precarious structuralizations that have been achieved. The child, in other words, becomes vulnerable to *self-fragmentation* because his affect states have not been met with the requisite responsiveness from the caregiving surround and thus cannot become integrated into the organization of his self-experience. Defenses against affect then become necessary to preserve the integrity of a brittle self-structure.

It is the thesis of this chapter that selfobject functions pertain fundamentally to the affective dimension of self-experience, and that the need for selfobject ties pertains to the need for specific, requisite responsiveness to varying affect states throughout development. Kohut's (1971, 1977) conceptualizations of mirroring and idealized selfobjects can be viewed as very important special instances of this expanded concept of selfobject functions in terms of the integration of affect. His discovery of the developmental importance of phase-appropriate mirroring of grandiose-exhibitionistic experiences points, from our perspective, to the critical role of attuned responsiveness in the integration of affect states involving pride, expansiveness, efficacy, and pleasurable excitement. As Kohut has shown, the integration of such affect states is crucial for the consolidation of self-esteem and self-confident ambition. The importance of early experiences of oneness with idealized sources of strength, security, and calm, on the other hand, indicates the central role of soothing, comforting responses from caregivers in the integration of affect states involving anxiety, vulnerability, and distress. As also shown by Kohut, such integration is of great importance in the development of self-soothing capacities which, in turn, contribute vitally to one's anxiety tolerance and overall sense of well-being.

Kohut (1977) seemed himself to be moving toward a broadened selfobject concept in his discussion of two ways in which parents can respond to the affect states characteristic of the oedipal phase:

> The affectionate desire and the assertive-competitive rivalry of the oedipal child will be responded to by normally empathic parents in two ways. The parents will react to the sexual desires and to the competitive rivalry of the child by becoming sexually stimulated and counteraggressive, and, at the same time, they will react with joy and pride to the child's developmental achievement, to his vigor and assertiveness [p. 230].

Whether the oedipal period will be growth enhancing or pathogenic will depend on the balance that the child experiences between these two modes of parental response to his oedipal feelings:

> If the little boy, for example, feels that his father looks upon him proudly as a chip off the old block and allows him to merge with him and with his adult greatness, then his oedipal phase will be a decisive step in self-consolidation and self-pattern-firming, including the laying down of one of the several variants of integrated maleness. . . . If, however, this aspect of the parental echo is absent during the oedipal phase, the child's oedipal conflicts will, even in the absence of grossly distorted parental responses to the child's libidinal and aggressive strivings, take on a malignant quality. Distorted parental responses are, moreover, also likely to

> occur under these circumstances. Parents who are not able to establish empathic contact with the developing self of the child will, in other words, tend to see the constituents of the child's oedipal aspirations in isolation—they will tend to see . . . alarming sexuality and alarming hostility in the child instead of larger configurations of assertive affection and assertive competition—with the result that the child's oedipal conflicts will become intensified [pp. 234–235].

In these quotations Kohut not only emphasizes the importance of parental responsiveness to oedipal-phase affectionate and rivalrous feelings; in addition, by focusing on affectionate and rivalrous feelings he expands the affective domain requiring such responsiveness considerably beyond that which is implicit in his earlier, more delimited formulations of mirroring and idealizing selfobject ties.

Basch (1985), in a discussion of the earlier, sensorimotor phase, advances an argument closely similar to ours by expanding Kohut's (1971) original concept of mirror function as pertaining to archaic grandiosity to encompass broad areas of "affective mirroring." Drawing on the work of Stern (1984), he writes:

> Through affective attunement the mother is serving as the quintessential selfobject for her baby, sharing the infant's experience, confirming it in its activity, and building a sensorimotor model for what will become its self concept. Affect attunement leads to a shared world; without affect attunement one's activities are solitary, private, and idiosyncratic. . . . [I]f . . . affect attunement is not present or is ineffective during those early years, the lack of shared experience may well create a sense of isolation and a belief that one's affective needs generally are somehow unacceptable and shameful [p. 35].

Basch views the defenses that appear in treatment as resistances against affect[1] originating in an absense of early affect attunement.

We now wish to extend the expanded concept of selfobject func-

---

[1]Basch notes that, as early as 1915, Freud, too, had expressed the belief that defense was always against affect.

tions to certain other aspects of affective development that we believe are central to the structuralization of self-experience. These include: (1) affect differentiation and its relationship to self-boundary formation; (2) the synthesis of affectively discrepant experiences; (3) the development of affect tolerance and the capacity to use affects as self-signals; and (4) the desomatization and cognitive articulation of affect states.

AFFECT DIFFERENTIATION AND SELF-ARTICULATION

Krystal (1974), who has been most comprehensive in applying a psychoanalytic developmental perspective to affect theory, has pointed out that an important component in the developmental transformation of affects "involves their separation and differentiation from a common matrix" (p. 98). He has emphasized as well the critical importance of the mother's responsiveness in helping the child to perceive and differentiate his varying affect states. What we wish to emphasize here is that this early affect-differentiating attunement to the small child's feeling states contributes vitally to the progressive articulation of his self-experience. Such differentiating responsiveness to the child's affects, therefore, constitutes a central selfobject function of the caregiving surround, in establishing the earliest rudiments of self-definition and self-boundary formation (see chapter 4).

The earliest processes of self-demarcation and individualization thus require the presence of a caregiver who, by virtue of a firmly structured sense of self and other, is able reliably to recognize, distinguish, and respond appropriately to the child's distinctive affect states. When a parent cannot discriminate and respond appropriately to feeling states of the child—for example, when those states conflict with a need for the child to serve the parent's own selfobject needs—then the child will experience severe derailments of his self-development. In particular, such situations will seriously obstruct the process of self-boundary formation, as the child feels compelled to "become" the selfobject that the parent requires (Miller, 1979) and thus to subjugate or dissociate central affective qualities of his own that conflict with this requirement (see Atwood and Stolorow, 1984, chapter 3, for a detailed clinical illustration).

THE SYNTHESIS OF AFFECTIVELY DISCREPANT EXPERIENCES

A second critical selfobject function of the early caregiving surround concerns the child's synthesis of contradictory affective experiences, a process vital to the establishment of an integrated sense of self. These early affect-synthesizing processes require the presence of a caregiver who, by virtue of firmly integrated perceptions, is able reliably to accept, tolerate, comprehend, and eventually render intelligible the child's intense, contradictory affect states as issuing from a unitary, continuous self. When a parent, in contrast, must perceive the child as "split"—for example, into one being whose "good" affects meet the selfobject needs of the parent and a second, alien being whose "bad" affects frustrate those needs—then the development of the child's affect-synthesizing capacity and the corresponding advance toward integrated selfhood will be severely obstructed, as affectively discrepant experiences become enduringly sequestered from one another in conformity with the parent's fragmentary perceptions (see Atwood and Stolorow, 1984, chapter 3, for a clinical illustration).

AFFECT TOLERANCE AND THE USE OF AFFECTS AS SELF-SIGNALS

Closely related to the role of early selfobject experiences in the processes of affect differentiation and synthesis and the corresponding differentiations and syntheses of self-experience is the contribution of the early caregiving surround to the development of affect tolerance and the capacity to use affects as signals to oneself (Krystal, 1974, 1975). These developmental attainments, too, require the presence of a caregiver who can reliably distinguish, tolerate, and respond appropriately to the child's intense, shifting affective states. It is the caregiver's responsiveness that gradually makes possible the modulation, gradation, and containment of strong affect, a selfobject function alluded to in the concept of the parent as a "stimulus barrier" or "protective shield" against psychic trauma (Krystal, 1978), in Winnicott's (1965) notion of the "holding environment," and in Bion's (1977) evocative metaphor of the container and the contained. This modulation and containment of affects make possible their use as self-signals. Rather than traumatically rupturing the continuity of self-experience, affects can thereby become employed in the service of its preservation.

Through countless experiences throughout early development, the caregiver, by comprehending, interpreting, accepting, and responding empathically to the child's unique and constantly shifting feeling states, is at the same time enabling him to monitor, articulate, and understandingly respond to them on his own. When the caregiver is able to perform this important selfobject function by way of using her own affect-signaling capacity, a process of internalization occurs, culminating in the child's ability to use his own emotional reactions as self-signals (see Tolpin, 1971, and Krystal, 1974, 1975). When affects are perceived as signals of a changing self-state rather than as indicators of impending psychological disorganization and fragmentation, the child is able to tolerate his emotional reactions without experiencing them as traumatic. Thus some rudimentary capacity to use affects as self-signals is an important component of the capacity to tolerate disruptive feelings when they emerge. Without this self-signaling capacity, affects tend to herald traumatic states (Krystal, 1978) and are thus disavowed, dissociated, repressed, or encapsulated through concrete behavioral enactments, self-protective efforts that literally cut off whole sectors of the child's affective life. In such cases, the emergence of affect often evokes painful experiences of shame and self-hatred, arising originally from the absence of positive, affirming responsiveness to the child's feelings. Emotionality thereby comes to be experienced as a solitary and unacceptable state, a sign of a loathsome defect within the self that must somehow be eliminated. Trauma is viewed here not as an event or series of events overwhelming an ill-equipped "psychic apparatus." Rather, the tendency for affective experiences to create a disorganized (i.e., traumatic) self-state is seen to originate from early faulty affect attunement, with a lack of mutual sharing and acceptance of affect states, leading to impaired affect tolerance and an inability to use affects as self-signals.

THE DESOMATIZATION AND COGNITIVE ARTICULATION OF AFFECT

Krystal (1974, 1975) has stressed that an important dimension of affect development (and we would add, of self development) is the evolution of affects from their early form as predominantly somatic states into experiences that can gradually be verbally articulated. He also emphasized the role of the caregiver's ability to identify correctly and verbalize the child's early affects in contributing to this developmental process. In our view, the importance of empathically attuned verbal articulation is not merely that it helps the child put his feelings into words; more fundamentally, it gradually facilitates the integration of affective states into *cognitive-affective schemata*—psychological structures that, in turn, contribute significantly to the organization and consolidation of the self. The caregiver's verbal articulations of the child's initially somatically experienced affects thus serve a vital selfobject function in promoting the structuralization of self-experience.

The persistence of psychosomatic states and disorders in adults may be seen as remnants of arrests in this aspect of affective and self development. When there is an expectation that more advanced, cognitively elaborated organizations of affective experience will not be met with the requisite responsiveness, replicating the faulty affect attunement of the childhood surround, the person may revert to more archaic, somatic modes of affect expression in the unconscious hope of thereby evoking the needed responses from others. Such psychosomatic states thus represent an archaic, presymbolic pathway of affect expression through which the person unconsciously attempts to establish a selfobject tie required for affect containment and thus for the maintenance of self-integrity. In the psychoanalytic situation we regularly observe that when the analyst becomes established as an affect-articulating and containing selfobject, the psychosomatic symptoms tend to recede or disappear, only to recur or intensify when the selfobject tie becomes disrupted or when the patient's confidence in the analyst's receptivity to his affects becomes significantly shaken.

IMPLICATIONS FOR PSYCHOANALYTIC THERAPY

Two major therapeutic implications follow from our expanded concept of selfobject functions as pertaining to the integration of affect, and from our corresponding emphasis on the fundamental importance for the structuralization of the self of the responsiveness of the early caregiving surround to the child's emerging affect states. One implication concerns the analytic approach to defenses against affects when these emerge as resistances in the course of psychoanalytic treatment.

As we have stressed, the need to disavow, dissociate, or otherwise defensively encapsulate affect arises originally in consequence of the failure of the early milieu to provide the requisite, phase-appropriate attunement and responsiveness to the child's emotional states. When such defenses against affect arise in treatment, they must be understood as being rooted in the patient's expectation or fear in the transference that his emerging feeling states will meet with the same faulty responsiveness that they received from the original caregivers. Further implications of this formulation for the analysis of conflict and resistance are discussed in the next two chapters.

A second therapeutic implication of our thesis concerning affects and selfobjects is that once the transference resistances against affect based on the "dread to repeat" (Ornstein, 1974) the damaging childhood experiences have been sufficiently analyzed (in the context of "good-enough" affective attunement on the part of the analyst), the patient's arrested developmental need for the originally absent or faulty responsiveness to his emerging affect states will be revived with the analyst. The specific emotional states involved and the specific functions that the patient requires the analyst to serve in relation to these states will determine the particular features of the unfolding selfobject transference. The analyst's ability to comprehend and interpret these feeling states and corresponding selfobject functions as they enter the transference will be critical in facilitating the analytic process and the patient's growth toward an analytically expanded and enriched affective life. It follows from this formulation that when remnants of early selfobject failure have become prominent in structuring the analytic relationship, a central curative element may be found in the selfobject transference bond itself and its pivotal role in the articulation, integration, and developmental transformation of the patient's affectivity.

In order to exemplify our thesis concerning affects and selfobjects, we turn now to a consideration of the integration of depressive affect.

THE INTEGRATION OF DEPRESSIVE AFFECT

Depressive affect states, such as sadness, grief, remorse, disappointment, and disillusionment, have many origins, meanings, and functions. Our focus here is on how and under what circumstances depressive affect is tolerated and integrated throughout development.

Our assumption is that all affects, in this case depressive affect, undergo development in concert with the consolidation and structuralization of the self. Such affect integration has its earliest rudiments in the sensorimotor phase, in the specific responsiveness to the child's affect states that serves to facilitate full emotional growth and development.

Depressive affect is integrated into the structure of the self through consistent, reliable, empathic attunement. When such attunement is chronically absent or faulty, such affect may herald a breakup of the cohesion and stability of the self-organization. The capacity to identify and withstand depressive feelings without a corresponding loss of self, fear of self-dissolution, or tendency to somatize the affect has its origins in the early affect-relatedness between the child and primary caregiver. A process of mourning and grief following loss or separation can occur only if depressive affects can be identified, comprehended, and tolerated. The ability to integrate depressive affect is therefore related to early affect attunement, which, in turn, lends definition to the child's experience of himself, solidifying self-boundaries. Depressive *disorders* (as distinct from depressive affect states) are rooted in early selfobject failure, leading to an inability to integrate depressive feelings and a corresponding derailment of self-development.

Kohut (1971, 1977) has shown that the child's (or developmentally arrested patient's) phase-appropriate experiences of gradual disillusionment with idealized images of himself and his primary objects constitute critical milestones in the structuralization of the self. As an alternative to Kohut's concept of "optimal frustration," we are contending here that it is not solely or even primarily the "quantity" of the accompanying depressive affects that determines whether they will be experienced as traumatic and self-disintegrative or as tolerable and capable of being integrated into the evolving self-organization. We believe that what is crucial to the child's (or patient's) growing capacity to integrate his sadness and his painful disappointments in himself and others is the reliable presence of a calming, understanding caregiver, irrespective of the "amount" or intensity of the affects involved.[2] When

---

[2]We are objecting here to the concept of "optimal frustration" because of its retention of economic and quantitative metaphors that are remnants of drive theory. For example, when Kohut (1971) describes an optimal frustration of the child's idealizing need as one in which "the child can experience disappointments with one idealized as-

the caregiver is able to tolerate, absorb, and contain the child's depressive affect states, which presupposes that they do not threaten the organization of *her* sense of self, she then functions to "hold the situation" (Winnicott, 1965) so that it can be integrated. Optimally, if such responsiveness is consistently present, the caregiver's selfobject functions gradually become internalized in the form of a capacity for self-modulation of depressive affect and an ability to assume a comforting, soothing attitude toward oneself. Consequently, such affect will not entail irretrievable losses in the self. The expectation that restitution will follow disruption becomes structuralized, providing the basis for a sense of self-continuity and confident hope for the future.

When a parent cannot tolerate the child's depressive feelings—because they do not conform to her own affect states, self-organization requirements, or selfobject needs—then she will be unable to assist the child in the critical task of affect integration. When the child experiences such protracted derailments of affect attunement, he may, in order to safeguard the needed tie, blame his own depressive feelings for the selfobject failure, resulting in a pervasive, self-hating helplessness and hopelessness or—if he responds by defensively dissociating the "offending" affects—in lifelong states of emptiness. It is here, we believe, that one can find the origins of chronic depressive disorder. Such patients in analysis resist the emergence of their depressive feelings for fear that once again they will be met with the same faulty responsiveness experienced in early childhood.

CLINICAL ILLUSTRATION

Steven began treatment at the age of 26 with a vague and generalized sense of doom and a pervasive fear that there was something terribly wrong with him. His fears centered specifically on his dread of becom-

---

pect or quality of the object after another" (p. 50) rather than with the total object, or one in which the shortcomings of the object "are of tolerable proportions" (p. 64), he places his emphasis on the "size" of the disappointment—and, by implication, the "amount" of the depressive affect—as the decisive factor that determines whether the disappointment will be pathogenic or growth-enhancing. In contrast, we are claiming that what is decisive is the responsiveness of the milieu to the child's depressive (and other) reactions. We are thus shifting the emphasis from "optimal frustration" to the centrality of affect attunement.

ing depressed, which he associated with "loss of control" over his mind and body. He complained of insomnia, failing graduate school grades, an inability to concentrate, and constant exhaustion from "covering over depression." Two events had precipitated his first visit to a psychotherapist: the broken engagement to his girlfriend of three years and the unexpected hospitalization of his mother. These two powerfully upsetting events took place on the same day three weeks before treatment had begun.

From the first session, Steven was extremely sensitive to the therapist's verbal and nonverbal reactions to him. He was usually very serious and occasionally quite anxious and agitated during the sessions. He had extreme difficulty focusing on what he wanted to communicate and his conversation often took on a distinctly dry and unconnected flavor, revealing no apparent depth of feeling. He spoke incessantly about the "traumas" he had suffered—not only recently but throughout his life—yet he was unable to provide any details of the events nor recall how they made him feel. All he knew was that his life was "not quite right." Any attempt to look more deeply into this problem would create an acute sense of anxiety, panic, and confusion, occasionally accompanied by dizziness, which then made him believe that he must have a "defective core" (that is, be psychotic).

He was intensely frightened that he would ultimately become massively depressed, since he believed his "defenses were failing" him. He knew he was depressed, but he "couldn't feel it." He remembered that once before he had "given in" to his feelings and had become so depressed that he had believed that he would never recover. Steven associated this belief with a "downward spiral" into a dark, deep hole, a process that, once begun, could never be reversed. In general, this is how Steven conceived of his depressive states. Consequently, he could neither express nor fully experience them until long into the treatment.

Steven had been employed as a computer programmer after dropping out of graduate school. He held many other odd jobs, filling his days and evenings with perpetual work. His obsessional style and lack of connection with his emotional life were the most salient features of the early months of therapy. He desperately wanted to communicate an exact account of what he had experienced and he showed an acute sensitivity to whether or not he was being understood. He explained that fears of being found "incorrect" or "inaccurate" were at the root of his anxiety, but it soon became clear that he believed that his feeling states, to the extent that he experienced them at all, were unacceptable and would ultimately drive the therapist away from him and destroy the therapeutic relationship. The growing tie to the therapist was therefore continually in jeopardy. He believed that the preservation of the tie depended upon his never making a "mistake," which was later understood to mean that he must not express any feelings that were not in line with what he perceived the therapist required and, more importantly, that might disturb her or make her feel inadequate. Thus, he was very compliant with the therapist's interventions, but his responses were strikingly devoid of affect. He was terrified that any spontaneous feelings that might be disjunctive with the therapist's state of mind would be rejected by her and have a disorganizing impact on him. When an intense emotional reaction was evoked, he would become confused and panicky, seeming to be unaware that he was experiencing an emotional reaction and thus completely unable to recognize its significance as a signal to himself. After Steven had become able to express some feelings in the therapeutic situation, he nevertheless remained continually baffled by what he "should do with them" now that he felt them. "I don't know what I feel, if I feel at all . . . if this is what a feeling is!"

Additionally, Steven was convinced that while on the surface the therapist might appear to accept his feelings, nonetheless she would secretly feel hatred, disgust, and loathing for him—especially, he said, because "they represent my feelings toward women." Steven had never experienced a deep inner sense of trust in another person and consequently was unable to believe that the therapist was not using him to fulfill her own needs, as his mother had continually done throughout his development. This lack of trust was pervasive early in the treatment and increased his vulnerability to almost intolerable proportions.

Steven's early life was punctuated by pervasive feelings of loneliness and emotional isolation. He had few friends as a young boy, "preferring" instead to spend countless hours with his mother in what appeared to be an intensely enmeshed relationship. Throughout his life he fantasized that his only purpose in life was to take care of his mother and try to extricate her from her recurrent, prolonged states of depression. She emerged in his memories as a cynical, pessimistic, suspicious, and severely hypocondriacal woman. Most of his memories of his early experiences were vague and fragmented but, as treatment progressed, he recalled a number of times when his mother was hospitalized for a variety of physical and psychiatric conditions, which left him in continual despair. Her first prolonged hospitalization took place when Steven was two, and she was hospitalized almost yearly throughout his childhood. Steven had both disavowed his affective reactions to these hospitalizations and repressed his knowledge of the reasons for them. In light of what was learned in the treatment about the mother's psychological state, it seems probable that many of these hospitalizations were for psychotic depressions. Steven recalled that his mother had been depressed as far back as he could remember, yet he had no conscious awareness of her psychological unavailability, nor did he recognize its impact on him.

Steven's disavowed childhood feelings of loss and abandonment were powerfully replicated when his girlfriend unexpectedly broke off their engagement. The depressive feelings that were evoked had a disorganizing impact on him and were, he felt, completely ignored by those around him. His mother was in the hospital attending to her own needs and his father remained as unavailable and stoney as Steven had always remembered him. In treatment he could not understand why he was unable to "get over" her and thus attacked himself mercilessly for this "defect" in himself. A few months into the therapy Steven recalled that he had been getting "deeper and deeper into depression" following the breakup. "'I felt as though it was spiraling downward. I began to get depressed and it continued on where I didn't want to do anything. I had no interest. I had an intense desire not to feel and not to think. It's a slightly suicidal tendency that scares me."

Steven clearly had no capacity to integrate his depressive feelings following this traumatic experience of loss, nor was he capable of accepting these affects in himself. He believed that they surely must mean that he was "crazy," for no one else understood them. Throughout his life, experiences of disappointment and sadness went unrecognized as far back as he could remember. He firmly believed that his mother could not tolerate his sadness and he remembered that she often ridiculed and berated him for feeling at all. When close childhood friends moved out of Steven's neighborhood—a trauma Steven repeatedly suffered—both his parents would laugh at his distress, commenting on what a "joke" it was that he was so upset. Not surprisingly, in light of such early experiences, Steven was extremely sensitive to any laughter or light-heartedness on the part of the therapist; he believed that she was ridiculing him for his feeling states as his parents had.

Steven's parents, particularly his father, had major difficulties maintaining stable relationships with others. Steven pictured his father as a reckless, self-involved man, unpredictable in both his personal and professional life, and "completely unconcerned about other people's feelings." His father abused his mother and often became absorbed in grandiose and immoral financial schemes. This left Steven with strong, conflictual feelings about him. He felt a strong desire not to believe that his father was the unethical and uncaring man he was portrayed to be and, at the same time, was filled with anger, disgust, and extreme disappointment in him. His father was incapable of recognizing how disorganizing these experiences were for his son and instead became annoyed and angry that the boy doubted his moral character.

Steven had lacked the kind of relationship he had needed with a father whom he could genuinely admire. His father's use of him to mirror his own grandiosity was prominent in Steven's recollections of their increasingly limited interactions. "He would sit me down to have father-son talks and he would go on and on. But there was one crucial thing missing. He was talking for himself, to himself, not to me. I was more of an object than another person." Steven's experience of his father as "distant," "erratic," and "unreachable" led eventually to his conviction at the age of 12 that there was no longer any hope for their relationship.

Even though Steven had little conscious awareness of his reactions to his mother's severe and repetitive depressions, his low self-esteem and propensity to become disorganized by affect states of all degrees of intensity can be assumed to be products of prolonged enmeshment with a mother who was chronically depressed and unresponsive, compounded by the lack of a stable bond with his father. Steven's own disavowed depressive affect states can be seen as a natural response to being chronically unresponded to. He shamefully admitted that he had been "depressed his whole life" but was "never able to feel it." He experienced "no zest for life, no glory in life," only a deep sense of isolation.

Steven's fears of his own depressive affects held a prominent place in the treatment for a long period of time. Initially he was somewhat aware of his dread of depressive feelings, believing that once he "got in touch with them" they would ultimately destroy him. He feared that he would fall into a "dark hole," never to return again, a fear that left him forever empty, helpless, and hopeless about his future. He believed that once he allowed himself to feel the massive disappointment, sadness, and remorse that had always lain beneath the surface, he would "go crazy" and end up like his psychotically depressed mother. Thus, his dread of feeling and acknowledging his depressive affects was based in part on his strong identification with, and incomplete differentiation from, his mother. In addition, the mother's own extreme vulnerability to depressive reactions rendered her unable to provide any sustained, attuned responsiveness to *his* depressive feelings. Any such reaction on Steven's part was met with ridicule, negation, angry scolding, or superficial apologies that left him feeling not responded to, worthless, deflated, unacceptable, and empty. His parents were unable either to understand or to tolerate his unhappiness; they considered any such affect as a vicious attack on their self-esteem and efficacy as parents.

During his many visits to his mother's hospital bedside throughout his childhood, Steven often felt extremely upset and frightened about losing her and being left alone. On such occasions, she could focus only on herself and how she was feeling, communicating to him clearly that what he was feeling was unimportant and unacceptable and that his affect state must somehow correspond to her needs. Nor could he at such times turn to his father, who always seemed too preoccupied with his own grandiose schemes and fantasies to respond to his son's distress. The emotional unavailability of his father exacerbated Steven's depressive feelings and intensified his enmeshment with his mother. No collateral pathway for affect integration was available. Steven thus came to believe that his depressive feelings were loathsome imperfections in himself. Since painful aspects of his subjective life could not be tolerated by his parents, he developed a firmly embedded conviction that painful affect must be "eliminated" and that "hurt must not be allowed."

Whenever Steven dared to show his emotions, his mother would accuse him of being too self-absorbed, like his father, and uncaring about the feelings of others, meaning principally her own. Her responses to his depressive feelings were always in terms of how they related to her own vulnerabilities and needs at the moment. She subtly communicated to him her own fear that his depressive feelings would lead to a psychotic regression as they had with her. Steven felt continuously alienated from his parents and peers alike. He eventually portrayed his childhood as lacking in any true, genuine feelings except pervasive emptiness and hopeless despair, coupled with a constant struggle to "survive just one more day." He commented often that "each man makes his own purgatory that he must live in," implying that *he* was fully to blame for his despair.

Steven's early memories were sparse and unarticulated, a phenomenon consistent with his massive early dissociation of affect, a product of the relentless lack of attunement to his depressive feeling states. He referred often to what he called the "missing links" in his history and in himself, imagery that was later understood to concretize the emotional disconnectedness he had experienced throughout his development. He spoke of life events as if they had happened to someone else and found it difficult to imagine that he was the same person now that he had been earlier in his childhood. Thus Steven lacked an experience of himself as being continuous in time, because he lacked the organizing and stabilizing influence of integrated affects that solidify the experience of being the same person though in the midst of change. In the therapy, Steven would occasionally feel a loss of a "time frame," especially during separations from the therapist or at the end of a session. Forty-five minutes would seem like ten, and four-day separations like months.

Previous to the crisis situation that brought Steven to treatment, he had been a most obedient son, especially in relation to his mother. When the mother would find herself in intolerable social and professional situations she would rely on her "bright, creative, and compliant" child to rescue her and "fix" what she had done wrong. Steven had become a very religious Catholic following his parents' divorce when he was eight, channeling all his energies into his religiosity. In this way he found an added source of structure for his increasingly chaotic inner world. His terrifying emotional reactions to countless disturbing childhood experiences (especially his parents' divorce and his mother's hospitalizations) were dissociated and repressed, solidifying his obsessional, cerebral character style. A state of pure, affectless intellectuality became his self-ideal of perfection, embodied in his intense idealization of the Star Trek character Mr. Spock, whose life seem completely free of the "imperfections of emotions." His struggle to attain this affectless ideal became poignantly clear as the treatment began to bring forth hitherto disavowed aspects of his emotional life.

For Steven, depressive affects of all degrees of intensity had become embedded in specific, dangerous meaning-contexts and consequently had remained a source of powerful anxiety throughout his life. In reaction to his mother's last hospitalization and being "dropped" by his girlfriend, he was unable to maintain his defenses against affect. An understanding of the dangers involved in acknowledging and expressing his depressive feelings evolved gradually in the course of treatment, finally centering on two separate but related dreaded outcomes. One was the expectation that his feelings would lead to further disorganization in his mother, completely precluding any accepting, affect-integrating responsiveness on her part. The other was his belief that, in the context of his merged relationship with her, he too would become psychologically disorganized, a hopelessly disintegrated self. Thus the emergence of depressive affect immediately triggered acute anxiety.

To summarize, Steven's inability to integrate depressive affect into his self-organization was seen to result both from profound selfobject failure in relation to his states of sadness, grief, and disappointment and from his deeply embedded association of depressive affect with the specter of disintegration—of both the self and the maternal object.

Steven's transference relationship with the therapist quickly replicated with distinct clarity his tie with his mother. He was in constant fear that the therapist would see him as a fragile, disintegration-prone person who was at the brink of psychosis when he expressed any depressive feelings. He was afraid to tell the therapist his dreams, being convinced that she then would clearly see the "crazy," disorganized qualities of his thoughts and feelings. Additionally, he was frightened of any depressive moods in the therapist for fear that she, like his mother and himself, would "lose control" and become psychotic. When Steven perceived a change of mood in the therapist, he would begin to feel anxious, as if it were he experiencing it. He believed that the therapist's failures and mistakes, like his mother's, were his own, and he felt her limitations as fatal flaws in himself. This incomplete self-object differentiation, in turn, made it all the more necessary to disavow any feelings of disappointment in the transference.

When depressive affects were evoked in Steven along with the corresponding states of acute anxiety, the therapist focused on the specific meaning-contexts and dreaded repetitions of early selfobject failure to which these feelings were linked. Whenever possible, she clarified his fears that she, like his mother, would find his feelings intolerable and unacceptable and would thus respond to them with spreading panic or angry belittlement, or become emotionally disturbed herself. Through this repeated analysis in the transference of Steven's resistances to depressive affect and the anticipated, extreme dangers that made them necessary, the therapist gradually became established for him as a person who would comprehend, accept, tolerate, and aid him in integrating these feelings, regardless of their intensity. Four closely interrelated consequences followed from this consolidation of the selfobject dimension of the transference. The first was that Steven began to show a much greater ability to recover painful memories of his past. The second was that he began to feel and express formerly dissociated feelings of deep, suicidal despair. Despite the painfulness of these feelings, the therapist and patient were able to understand that they reflected a developmental step in affect integration.

A third consequence, following from the second, was the crystallization of his conviction that his emerging depressive feelings constituted a deadly threat to others—a remnant of countless early experiences in which he perceived that his sadness and disappointment were experienced by his mother as psychologically damaging. This theme was dramatically symbolized in dreams that followed immediately upon the disclosure of his suicidal feelings. In the imagery of these dreams, he portrayed his emerging feeling states as uncontrollable destructive forces that, once unleashed, would engulf and annihilate everyone around him.

Not unexpectedly, Steven's belief that his depressive affects were dangerous and destructive to others began to dominate the transference as he became frightened that his feelings would inflict psychological harm upon the therapist. As this fear was repeatedly analyzed in the transference, its genetic roots in his mother's extreme vulnerabilities and consequent inability to tolerate and "hold" his depressive affects became clarified in increasingly bold relief. This ongoing transference analysis, together with Steven's progressively solidifying new experience of the therapist's affect attunement and containment, made it possible for him not only to experience and express previously dissociated depressive feelings, but to begin to reunite with ever-widening spheres of his affectivity in general and, in turn, to move toward an experience of himself as an emotionally complex human being.

The fourth consequence of the consolidation of the selfobject transference tie and the corresponding expansion of Steven's affective life was that he showed increasing capacity to immerse himself in intensely *pleasurable* experiences, most notably those that emerged at this time in his first sexual relationship with a woman. Analysis of his *fears* of experiencing and disclosing these pleasurable feelings provided insights into the impact on Steven of his mother's inclusion of him in her own paranoid view of the world. He remembered that his mother had told him repeatedly that she had brought him up with the overriding aim of providing him with "tools for survival"—that the world was a "very dangerous place" and that he must devote his life to the protection of himself. She conveyed her belief that feelings must not be expressed—or even felt—because they indicated to her a loss of self-control, which interrupted his concentration on self-protection, thereby rendering him vulnerable to annihilation. His positive affect states were subject to the same maternal restrictions as were his negative ones. Steven recalled only a "few moments" when his mother allowed him to feel joy and unburdened pleasure in what he happened to be immersed in as a young boy. During these times, when he began to feel the normal expansiveness of fearless pleasure in mastery, his mother would soon become alarmed and warn him that he must not give up "preparation for tomorrow's dangers for happiness today." This theme was clearly replicated in the transference in Steven's expectation of the therapist's "severe disapproval" as he began to express his newfound feelings of excitement, happiness, and carefree self-involvement. He would refer to these states as "reckless abandon" for which he expected punishment—for example, when he disclosed to the therapist the enormous satisfaction and pride he experienced in his first sexual encounter. Working through these fears of retribution in the transference, and clarifying their origins in his mother's ever-vigilant alertness to danger, strengthened the selfobject tie to the therapist, further expanding Steven's capacity to experience strong feeling.

A vivid example of Steven's progress in affect tolerance arose in the context of his decision to relocate to a distant city in order to resume his education at the only graduate school at which he was accepted. He was immediately able to experience and express acute feelings of sadness and distress over the impending loss of the therapist—feelings that earlier would have had to be disavowed because of their links with early traumatic selfobject failure in this area. The understanding and acceptance of these painful depressive affect states led to two final important therapeutic transformations, the first consisting of a newly formed dimension to the transference. Steven began to feel the loss of a "true friendship," a kind of bond he had never before felt was possible given the lack of genuineness of past relationships in his life, beginning with those he had with his parents. Such increased feelings of closeness and trust came as a direct result of Steven's growing awareness that his affect states, regardless of whether they were positive or negative, could now be understood, tolerated, and rendered intelligible by the therapist. It is notable that this new feeling of friendship crystallized shortly after intense depressive feelings had been fully expressed to the therapist. The bond had been further solidified by the affect-integrating responsiveness of the therapist, increasing Steven's sense of being worthy of her friendship.

The second consequence of the integration of Steven's feelings of loss was an unexpected illumination of his heretofore unarticulated perception of his *father's* emotional states. He remembered for the first time that not only was his mother chronically depressed throughout his early years, but his father too had suffered from prolonged depressions that were punctuated by extreme agitation. "I grew up believing that depression was a way of life, that there was nothing else." Steven had long attempted to avoid identification with either parent for fear of becoming like them. Since neither parent was available to provide any consistent responsiveness to his affect states, he had remained arrested in his affective development and had become increasingly enmeshed in a futile attempt to alleviate his mother's pain and suffering. In the transference, the therapist had eventually become established as the affect-integrating selfobject that Steven had sorely missed throughout his formative years. During the course of therapy, he seemed gradually to internalize the therapist's integrative attunement to his emergent feeling states and increasingly to identify with her accepting, understanding attitude toward his previously disavowed affective life. Steven's stalled emotional growth was thereby permitted to resume once again.

CONCLUSION

Selfobject functions pertain fundamentally to the integration of affect into the evolving organization of self-experience. This conceptualization brings into sharpened focus the critical developmental importance of reliable affect attunement from the caregiving surround in assisting the child in the tasks of differentiating, synthesizing, modulating, and cognitively articulating his emergent emotional states, affect-integrating functions which, in turn, contribute vitally to the structuralization of his sense of self. We exemplified this thesis by focusing on the necessary integrations of depressive affect throughout development and by presenting a clinical illustration of severe selfobject failure in this area. As our case example demonstrates, a focus on affect integration and its failures holds important implications for both the analytic approach to resistance and the understanding of the curative action of selfobject transferences. Our focus on "interaffectivity" and its derailments also brings into clear view the specific intersubjective contexts that facilitate or obstruct the process of self development.

6

Developmental Failure and Psychic Conflict

Psychoanalytic psychologies of developmental deficit and of psychic conflict are often regarded as antithetical to one another or, at best, as complementary (Kohut, 1977). It is our thesis in this chapter that the two sets of phenomena are closely interrelated and that inner conflict always takes form in specific intersubjective contexts of developmental derailment.

The centrality of inner conflict in human psychological life has been a fundamental tenet of psychoanalysis since its inception. In recent years, however, long-held assumptions about the nature and origins of conflict have increasingly become subject to critical reappraisal. Arguments put forth by a number of authors (Gill, 1976; Klein, 1976; Schafer, 1976; Stolorow, 1978) have persuasively demonstrated the extent to which the psychoanalytic understanding of conflict has been obstructed by classical metapsychology and, in particular, by the theory of instinctual drive. Proposals have been offered that would replace the mechanistic imagery of a mental apparatus disposing of drive energies with a psychology of conflict recast in the language of clashing personal purposes (Klein, 1976) and human actions (Schafer, 1976). It is our contention that from a psychoanalytic perspective conflict is always and only a subjective state of the individual person and that it is the task of psychoanalytic inquiry to illuminate the specific contexts of meaning in which such conflicts take form. We are thus proposing a strictly *psychological* approach to conflict, in line with Kohut's (1982) desire to reframe psychoanalysis as a pure psychology.

The frequently posed antithesis between conflict theory and Kohut's self psychology is, in our view, an artifact of the embeddedness of the traditional concept of conflict in classical metapsychology and drive theory. When conflict is freed from the encumbering image of an energy disposal apparatus and is pictured solely as a subjective state of the person, then the supposed antithesis between conflict theory and self psychology vanishes. When conflict is liberated from the doctrine of the primacy of instinctual drive, then the specific meaning-contexts that give rise to subjective states of conflict becomes an empirical question to be explored psychoanalytically. The focus of psychoanalytic inquiry then shifts from the presumed vicissitudes of drive to the intersubjective contexts in which conflict states crystallize, and to the impact of these contextual configurations on the person's psychological organization. Such a stance holds profound implications for one's *clinical* approach to conflicts that emerge in the psychoanalytic situation, a subject to which we return later.

Another advantage of viewing conflict solely as a subjective state of the person is that it invites a consideration of the developmental origins and, especially, the developmental *prerequisites* of particular conflict states (see Stolorow & Lachmann, 1980). In general it may be said that the experience of the self-in-conflict presupposes that some minimal degree of structuralization of the sense of self has been reliably achieved. Thus, in those disintegrative states in which the cohesion of self-experience becomes significantly lost and immersion in an archaic selfobject tie is required for its restoration, states of conflict between clashing motivational strivings will not predominate in the person's subjective field, because the imperative need to reestablish the required tie is experientially preeminent. When the required tie is reestablished, by contrast, and self-integrity thereby becomes restored, then inner conflict may emerge into prominence—for example, when central strivings and affective qualities of the person are believed to be inimical to the maintenance of the bond.[1]

Observations and reconstructions of self development suggest that it involves at least two overlapping processes (see Kohut, 1977; Atwood and Stolorow, 1984; Brandchaft, 1985; Wolf, 1980): (1) the consolidation of a nuclear sense of coherence and well-being, and (2) the differentiation of self from other and the corresponding establishment of an individualized array of guiding aspirations and ideals (see

[1]A similar conception of the origins of psychic conflict has been formulated independently by Herbert Linden (1983).

chapter 4). Critical to these structuralization processes is the attuned responsiveness of the caregiving surround to the child's evolving emotional states and needs. The child's needs for such specific responsiveness undergo a series of maturational shifts. Conflicts may arise and become structuralized at any point in this developmental progression. With regard to self-consolidation, such conflicts will revolve around the child's basic needs for mirroring responses and for connectedness to idealized sources of comfort and strength. With regard to self-differentiation, conflicts will center on the child's need for the continuance of selfobject ties that can serve as a source of affirming, facilitating, and solidifying support for his strivings for self-delineation and for the establishment of individualized goals and values. Under the influence of drive and tripartite structural theory, analysts have tended to interpret these conflicts as originating in oedipal and preoedipal drive fixations and their corresponding superego structures and forerunners. This concept of inevitably structuralized, instinctually derived conflict obscures the contextual configurations—the specific developmental asynchronies—from which such conflicts arise, thereby limiting and derailing analytic progress. We suggest that the understanding of emergent conflict is better served by recognizing that, at every phase of development, the structuralization of conflict is determined by the specific intersubjective field in which it is embedded, just as its resolution in analysis is determined by the intersubjective dialogue in which it reemerges.

If parents cannot adapt themselves to the changing needs of their developing child, then the chid will adapt himself to what is available in order to maintain the required ties. This, we believe, is the route by which inner conflict becomes structuralized and by which civilized man continues to exchange "a portion of his possibilities for happiness for a portion of security" (Freud, 1930, p. 115).

In a previous work (Stolorow, 1985), this thesis was exemplified through an examination of the origins of those subjective states that ordinarily are grouped under the heading of "superego conflict." Traditionally, the concepts of superego and superego conflict, and the attendant role of guilt in pathogenesis, have been formulated in terms of the metapsychological assumptions of classical drive theory. It was argued in the earlier paper that the experiential configurations covered by the terms "superego" and "superego conflict" originate in the child's perceptions of what is required of him to maintain the ties that are vital to his well-being. Once these requirements become structuralized as invariant organizing principles of the child's subjective world, he will be vulnerable to painful feelings of guilt, shame, or anxiety whenever his emotional strivings threaten to violate them.

Most often the requirements for maintaining needed ties involve the child's having to serve significant selfobject functions for his parents. When a parent consistently requires an archaic state of oneness with a child, for example, then the child's strivings for more differentiated selfhood become the source of severe conflict and guilt. In such instances, the child perceives that his acts of self-demarcation and unique affective qualities are experienced by the parent as psychologically damaging, often leading to the child developing a perception of himself as omnipotently destructive. This self-perception as a cruel and dangerous destroyer, originating in the parent's need for the child as an archaic selfobject, both obstructs the process of self-boundary formation and becomes an enduring source of guilt and self-punishment—the "harsh superego" and "sadistic superego forerunners" of classical theory.

We now wish to broaden and refine this conceptualizaton of conflict by elaborating a set of formulations concerning the central role played by failures of affect integration in the genesis and structuralization of inner conflict. In chapter 5, we wrote:

> An absence of steady, attuned responsiveness to the child's affect states creates minute but significant derailments of optimal affect integration and leads to a propensity to dissociate or disavow affective reactions because they threaten the precarious structuralizations that have been achieved. The child, in other words, becomes vulnerable to *self-fragmentation* because his affect states have not been met with the requisite responsiveness from the caregiving surround and thus cannot become integrated into the organization of his self-experience. Defenses against affect then become necessary to preserve the integrity of a brittle self-structure [p. 67].

Although the word "conflict" does not appear in this passage, we believe that it contains the essential ingredients for a psychoanalytic understanding of conflict formation. The specific intersubjective contexts in which conflict takes form are those in which central affect states of the child cannot be integrated because they fail to evoke the requisite attuned responsiveness from the caregiving surround. Such unintegrated affect states become the source of lifelong inner conflict, because they are experienced as threats both to the person's established psychological organization and to the maintenance of vitally needed ties. Thus affect-dissociating defensive operations are called into play, which reappear in the analytic situation in the form of resistance. A defensive self-ideal is often established, which represents the self purified of the "offending" affect states that were perceived as intolerable to the early surround (see the case of Steven, chapter 5), and the inability to fully embody this affectively purified ideal then becomes a continual source of shame and self-loathing. It is in the defensive walling off of central affect states, rooted in early derailments of affect integration, that the origins of what has traditionally been called the "dynamic unconscious" can be found.

A critical therapeutic implication of this formulation concerns the analytic approach to resistance. When defenses against affect arise in treatment, they must be understood as being rooted in the patient's expectation or fear *in the transference* that his emerging feeling states will meet with the same faulty responsiveness that they received from the original caregivers. Furthermore, these resistances against affect cannot be interpreted as resulting solely from intrapsychic processes within the patient. Such resistances are most often evoked by events occurring within the intersubjective dialogue of the analytic situation that for the patient signal the analyst's lack of receptivity to the patient's emerging feeling states and that therefore herald a traumatic recurrence of early selfobject failure (Ornstein, 1974). Thus, while the persistence of resistance reflects the continuing influence of preestablished organizing principles (the repetitive aspect of the transference), the resolution of resistance and the establishment of new modes of experiencing require careful analytic attention to the specific intersubjective contexts in which the defensive reactions arise and recede.

AFFECT STATES AND PSYCHIC CONFLICT

Two broad classes of affect states can be distinguished that regularly become sources of structuralized conflict in the context of early selfobject failure.

Developmental Strivings

One category encompasses those feeling states which accompany the child's strivings and developmental progress toward individualized selfhood (see chapter 4). Such indicators of developmental progress include feelings of pride, expansiveness, efficacy, and pleasure in oneself, as well as willful rebelliousness, emergent sexuality, and competitive aggressiveness. As Kohut (1971, 1977) has shown, the integration of such affect states through phase-appropriate mirroring is crucial for the consolidation of self-cohesion, self-esteem, and self-confident ambition. When such mirroring responsiveness is consistently absent, because the child's developmental strivings and accompanying affect states are injurious to the parent's sense of well-being, then such strivings and feeling states become the source of severe and enduring inner conflict and guilt.

Clinical Illustration: An Adolescent Crisis

Sally, a 17-year-old girl, was referred by her former therapist, a woman in her sixties, because the treatment had reached a stalemate. The patient was severely depressed, was relentlessly self-critical and self-attacking, thought frequently of killing herself, and was plagued by recurrent pains in her legs that apparently were of psychogenic origin. The referring therapist conceived of the patient's current intractable state as a manifestation of a "negative therapeutic reaction" rooted in severe resistance, masochism, and a highly sadistic superego.

Sally seemed to her new analyst to be an attractive and very intelligent youngster, self-reflective to a fault, and acutely attuned to the needs and feelings of others. The imperative that she incessantly please and satisfy others and sacrifice herself to their expectations quickly emerged as the dominant theme in her psychological life, an important element in the transference relationship with her former therapist that had gone unnoticed.

Sally's parents were divorced when she was four years old, after which her father became absorbed in an endless succession of short-lived affairs and showed little interest in his daughter. Her mother frequently disparaged him to Sally, and the patient herself recalled many humiliating incidents in which he had let her down—for example, failing to pay her school tuition bills and canceling scheduled visits with her at the last minute.

The loss of and severe disappointments by her father had the effect of greatly intensifying the bond between Sally and her mother. A central characteristic of this tie was that her mother, who was chronically depressed, had come to require a sense of oneness with Sally as an archaic selfobject—that is, Sally's unfailing, loving responsiveness and continual availability had become essential to the maintenance of her mother's feeling of well-being. Her mother thus experienced Sally's phase-appropriate strivings for individualized selfhood as a profound psychological injury and made Sally feel as if these developmental thrusts and accompanying feeling states were deliberate and cruel attempts to damage and destroy her. Not surprisingly, this pattern reached crisis proportions during Sally's adolescence, with her mother reacting to her emerging sexuality and growing interest in boys by dissolving in tears and jealous rages. Sally, in turn, felt unbearably guilty and became increasingly depressed, self-attacking, and suicidal.

Believing that the source of the patient's difficulties was to be found in conflicts over aggressive drive derivatives, her former therapist had begun to offer interpretations of Sally's presumed unconscious aggressive wishes, both in relation to her mother and in the transference. Sally's condition significantly worsened, leading the therapist, who was becoming increasingly alarmed, to make the referral to another analyst. It was reconstructed that the first therapist's interpretations of aggressive wishes were felt by Sally to replicate her mother's view of her as inherently cruel and destructive, and they therefore only exacerbated her guilty self-attacks and her resistance.

It soon became apparent that because of her mother's enmeshment with her as an archaic selfobject, Sally's strivings for greater self-demarcation had become the source of unbearable conflict and guilt for her. As the analyst repeatedly clarified for the patient how her mother reacted to her rebellious thrusts toward more differentiated selfhood as if they were expressions of destructive aggression, and how this was the principal reason for her guilt and self-attacks, her depression and other symptoms lifted, as her stalled adolescent development was permitted to resume. She was able to become involved with a steady boyfriend and to decide to go away to college, though her mother disapproved of both. In the transference, she had experienced the analyst as a deeply longed-for, idealizable, paternal selfobject, who helped her to free her affective life from the web of her mother's archaic needs and who aligned himself with her quest for a more distinct self-definition.

Not unexpectedly, Sally returned to analysis a year after her graduation from college. While the earlier brief course of treatment had helped to free her adolescent development from the grip of her mother's needs, she now found the early pattern of bondage to her mother becoming repeated in her professional and personal relationships. Her wrenching self-demarcation guilt and the corresponding perception of herself as a cruel destroyer (her "superego conflicts") had become structuralized by her early formative experiences with her mother as enduring features of her psychological life. These now became engaged in an intensive analytic process in which the primary, conflictual tie to the mother could be worked through directly in the transference, through consistent interpretation of Sally's expectations of adverse reactions in the analyst to her efforts at self-articulation.

Reactive Feeling States

The second broad class of affect states that regularly become sources of structuralized conflict includes all those painful and disruptive feeling states that are *reactive* to threats or injuries to the self and/or ruptures in a primary selfobject bond. As is implied in Kohut's (1971, 1977) emphasis on the developmental importance of experiences of oneness with idealized sources of strength and calm, a central selfobject function of the early surround pertains to the child's need for soothing, comforting, modulating, and containing responses to assist in the integration of such disruptive affect states as anxiety, sadness, disappointment, shame, guilt, and rage. It is this integrative responsiveness to the child's (or patient's) painful emotional reactions that helps to heal the narcissistic wounds, mends the broken ties, and permits the developmental process to proceed. In contrast, when such attuned responsiveness is consistently absent, because the child's reactive affect states threaten the parent's self-organization requirements, then the child's unintegrated painful feelings become the source of wrenching inner conflict, self-hatred, and a lifelong vulnerability to traumatic states (see chapter 5). In the analytic situation, such persons resist the emergence of painful affect for fear that once again it will be met with the same faulty responsiveness experienced in early childhood.

Clinical Illustration: Reactive Depressions

Tom was a 57-year-old man with considerable artistic endowment and, when he was functioning well, substantial charm. He had compensated for repeated failures in school by a prodigious regime of self-teaching and had acquired expertise not only in cultural and artistic matters, but also in such diverse fields as astronomy, anthropology, and history. He was, however, plagued by recurrent episodes of severe and paralyzing depression, which always followed some personal setback. One regular precipitant was his wife's depressive mood, which he always attributed to some failing of his own. A lack of psychological differentiation was also shown in his reactions to any extended physical separations from her, which produced profound disintegrative changes in his state of mind. To counteract these, he would engage in brief sexual affairs that served to restore a sense of aliveness and fend off frightening feelings of apathy and "deadness." Other triggering events for his depressions were unfavorable reviews of his work or contemporaries' being chosen over him for assignments or awards in his field.

In these reactive states he would feel "defeated," find it difficult to get out of bed, and experience a "black cloud" descending over him, along with a nearly complete loss of motivation. He would become beset with intense hypochondriacal worries, feel convinced that his creativity had left him, and brood obsessively about his impending financial demise. He would then sink into an orgy of self-recrimination for his state of mind, alternating with intense and virulent self-pity for the wretchedness of his existence. It soon became apparent that for Tom any trace of depressive affect was a source of severe conflict and ruthless self-attack.

Tom's mother emerged in his memories as an intensely anxious, childlike, and volatile woman, chronically disappointed with her passive and ineffectual husband. From the beginning, she was overburdened by the demands of her vigorous first child, Tom, and after 18 months left him in the care of her own inadequate parents, only to reclaim him two years later. His subsequent childhood years were marked by frequent scenes in which his mother would bitterly bemoan her fate in getting married and having children, immersing herself in dramatic displays of self-pity, especially when she was disappointed by Tom's maturational lags or failures in school. Often she would fall to the floor in a "dead" faint or retire to her room, pull down the shades, and remain in bed for long periods of time. In consequence of countless experiences such as these, Tom came to believe that his own painful disappointments in himself, as well as his depressive reactions to them, were a source of unbearable psychological injury for his mother.

In the analysis Tom could sustain no positive sense of self in the wake of his recurrent episodes of devitalization, regardless of the successes he had achieved. It became clear that his vicious self-reproaches, in reaction to disappointments and to the depressive moods to which his vulnerability exposed him, completely undermined his resilience and, in circular fashion, further exacerbated his depressive states.

After prolonged, detailed observation it became apparent that Tom consistently, if silently, perceived the analyst to be painfully disappointed in him and in himself whenever the patient felt depressed. Each depressive state was colored by the invariant meanings his moods had come to acquire—meaning-structures that now crystallized in the intersubjective context of the analytic dialogue, which revived critical pathogenic elements of his early tie to his mother. These meanings included Tom's belief that he was cursed with a fatal and unyielding defect (his vulnerability to depressive experiences), that he was completely unacceptable and unwanted as he was, and that his depressive feelings were a constant, painful reminder to his objects—now the analyst—of their own failures. Thus it could be seen that Tom's depressive experiences had been a lifelong source of conflict for him because of his deeply embedded conviction that the disclosure of such feelings was psychologically damaging to those on whom he relied.

This transference configuration invariably materialized with the first sapping of Tom's vitality. He would try desperately to restore his buoyancy, as well as the analyst's, by offering reassurances, but these would inevitably collapse beneath his (and, he believed, the analyst's) knowledge that he was only attempting to cover up the flaw he had once again exposed. Tom's ruthless self-reproaches (exemplary symptoms of a "harsh superego") now became comprehensible as urgent attempts to maintain his connectedness with the analyst, much as he had found it necessary to do with his mother, when he believed that his state of mind had become a source of unbearable disappointment for the analyst as it had been for his mother. Only by confessing his worthlessness could he in some measure absolve himself and restore the tie, joining the analyst in the latter's misfortune in having him for a patient.

Frequently patients who show symptoms such as these and who seem not to make progress in analysis are assumed to suffer from a basic conflict over depending on an object. It is further widely believed that such conflict originates in the intense destructiveness or envy that dependence mobilizes. Tom certainly experienced enormous conflict over his continued needs for objects, and this was an important source of his self-loathing. This conflict, however, was not rooted in an instinctually determined sadism. Rather, it stemmed from two central organizing principles of his subjective life. One was the degree of his vulnerability to separations, rejections, or criticism, a product of his arrested need for confirming and comforting selfobject ties. A second was the extent to which he believed that *he* must accept blame for any disjunctive experience in order to preserve the needed ties. He thus blamed his depressive reactions for the selfobject failures that produced them, with the result that his "hopeless flaws" seemed repeatedly and relentlessly confirmed.

Tom's mother could not tolerate or accept his sadness or disappointments, experiences that therefore could never become integrated or modulated. He was thus unable to learn to comfort himself when distressed, and his depressive moods remained a source of unyielding conflict and self-hatred throughout his life, until the pathogenic tie to his mother was reanimated, clarified, and worked through in the analytic dialogue.

CONCLUSION

A focus on affect integration and its derailments illuminates the complex interrelationships between developmental failure and the formation of psychic conflict, both in childhood and in the psychoanalytic situation. The specific intersubjective contexts in which conflict takes form are situations in which central affect states of the child cannot be integrated because they fail to evoke the requisite responsiveness from the caregiving surround. Such unintegrated feeling states become the source of enduring inner conflict, because they are experienced as threats both to the person's established psychological organization and to the maintenance of vitally needed ties. Two broad classes of affect states regularly become sources of structuralized conflict in the context of faulty affect attunement: those that accompany the child's developmental strivings and those that are reactive to injuries and disruptions. In treatment, the emergence of unintegrated affect is resisted for fear that the analyst will replicate the faulty responsiveness of the childhood milieu.

7

Thoughts on Psychoanalytic Cure

In an excellent historical survey, Lawrence Friedman (1978) traced the vicissitudes of the psychoanalytic theory of cure from Freud's writings on the subject to the views of contemporary thinkers. Emerging from Friedman's review were three factors that Freud believed to be important in achieving therapeutic benefits: (1) the provision of cognitive insight, (2) the affective bond to the analyst, and (3) the integration of formerly dissociated experiential contents. Friedman detected throughout Freud's work on the process of treatment a "running battle" between the respective claims of the first two of these factors, although, Friedman noted, "when one looks more closely one sees that it is not equal combat, but a struggle for survival on the part of understanding [that is, cognitive insight]" (p. 526). For example, Freud (1938) pointed to the positive transference as the most important curative agent.

Friedman's study demonstrates that subsequent discourse on the therapeutic action of psychoanalysis has been characterized by a continuation of this "running battle" between the respective claims of intellectual insight and affective attachment. Participants in the Marienbad Symposium on the Theory of Therapeutic Results in Psychoanalysis in 1936, for example, readily accepted Strachey's (1937) ideas about the introjection of the analyst's benign attitudes into the patient's superego functioning, a formulation that clearly placed the accent on the affective bond with the analyst and its internalization by the patient. On the other hand, participants in the Edinburgh Symposium on the Curative Factors in Psychoanalysis 25 years later reacted uneasily to Gitelson's (1962) implied claim that the affective relationship with the analyst can in itself produce structural changes. The other panelists at this conference forcefully reaffirmed the central therapeutic importance of cognitive insight as conveyed by interpretation.

Thus, the struggle initiated by Freud continues, with such writers as Loewald (1960), Stone (1961), Modell (1976), and Kohut (1977, 1984) emphasizing affective attachment, and others, such as Stein (1966), Kernberg (1975), and Curtis (1986), sounding the battle cry of insight through interpretation.

It is our belief that this long-standing debate over the role of insight versus attachment in psychoanalytic cure is symptomatic of a chronic malady that has pervaded not only psychoanalytic theory but Western psychology in general. We refer to the fragmentation of psychic reality that artificially sections human subjectivity into cognitive and affective domains. This false dichotomy has persisted in psychoanalytic self psychology as well. Kohut (1984), for example, divided the interpretive process into two phases, the first emphasizing empathic understanding based on affective attunement and the second emphasizing interpretive explanations based on cognitive inferences.

We contend that the significant psychological transformations that occur in psychoanalytic treatment always involve unitary configurations of experience in which cognitive and affective components are virtually indivisible. *Meaning*—the supreme category of psychoanalytic inquiry—is, after all, an indissociable amalgam of cognition and affect. Furthermore, the conceptualizations of selfobject transference and of the psychoanalytic situation as an intersubjective system provide a framework for recognizing that insight through interpretation, affective bonding through empathic attunement, and the facilitation of psychological integration are indissoluble facets of a unitary developmental process that we call psychoanalysis. For example, from the standpoint of the selfobject dimension of the transference, the therapeutic impact of the analyst's accurate interpretations lies not only in the insights they convey, but also in the extent to which they demonstrate the analyst's attunement to the patient's emotional states and developmental needs. The analyst's interpretations are not disembodied transmissions of insight *about* the analytic relationship. They are an inherent, inseparable component *of* that very bond, and their therapeutic action derives from the intersubjective matrix in which they crystallize.

Emerging from the formulations of selfobject functions, conflict, and resistance discussed in chapters 4, 5, and 6 is, in very broad brushstrokes, a *bipolar conception of transference* (see also A. Ornstein, 1974). At one pole of the transference is the patient's longing to experience the analyst as a source of requisite selfobject functions that were missing or insufficient during the formative years. In this dimension of the transference, the patient hopes and searches for a new selfobject experience that will enable him to resume and complete an arrested developmental process. At the other pole are the patient's expectations and fears of a transference repetition of the original experiences of selfobject failure. It is this second dimension of the transference that becomes the source of conflict and resistance.

We believe that a well-conducted psychoanalysis is characterized by inevitable, continual shifts in the figure-ground relationships between these two poles of the transference, as they oscillate between the experiential foreground and background of the treatment. These oscillations correspond to shifts in the patient's psychological organization and motivational priorities that occur in response to alterations in the tie to the analyst—shifts and alterations that are profoundly influenced by whether or not the analyst's interpretive activity is experienced by the patient as being attuned to his affective states and needs. For example, when the analyst is experienced as unattuned, foreshadowing a traumatic repetition of early selfobject failure, the conflictual and resistive dimension of the transference is frequently brought into the foreground, while the patient's selfobject yearnings are, of necessity, driven into hiding. On the other hand, when the analyst is able to analyze accurately the patient's experience of selfobject failure, demonstrating his attunement to the patient's reactive affect states and thereby mending the ruptured tie, the selfobject pole of the transference becomes restored and strengthened and the conflictual/resistive/repetitive dimension tends to recede into the background.[1]

It is our contention that the mode of therapeutic action of psychoanalysis differs depending on whether it is the selfobject or the conflictual dimension of the transference that occupies the position of foreground at any particular juncture of the treatment.

When the conflictual dimension is preeminent in the transference, an essential ingredient of the working through process concerns the in-

---

[1] At certain other times, the patient's experience of the analyst's attunement may *heighten* the conflictual and resistive aspect of the transference because it stirs the patient's walled off selfobject longings and archaic hopes, along with his dread of the retraumatization that he fears will follow from the exposure of these longings and hopes to the analyst (see the case of Martin, chapter 4).

terpretive illumination of the patient's unconscious organizing activity as discerned within the intersubjective dialogue between patient and analyst. We refer here to the ways in which the patient's experience of the analyst and his activities—especially his interpretive activity—is unconsciously and recurrently patterned by the patient according to developmentally preformed meanings and invariant themes, usually taking the form of expectations and fears of retraumatization. In *Structures of Subjectivity,* we conceptualized the therapeutic action of analyzing this unconscious structuring activity in the transference as a process of structural transformation. Like Friedman (1978), we found it useful to apply Piaget's (1954) principles of structural assimilation and accommodation:

> The repeated interpretive clarification of the nature, origins, and purposes of the configurations of self and object into which the analyst is assimilated, together with the repeated juxtaposition of these patterns with experiences of the analyst as a new object to which they must accommodate, both establish reflective knowledge of how the patient's perception of the analytic relationship is being shaped by his psychological structures, and at the same time invite the synthesis of alternative modes of experiencing the self and object world. As the ossified . . . forms that have heretofore structured the patient's experiences are progressively . . . reorganized, a new and enriched personal reality opens up before him, made possible by the newly expanded and reflectively conscious structures of his subjective world.
>
> Analysis thus introduces a new object into the patient's experience, an object unique in the capacity to invoke past images and yet also to demonstrate an essential difference from these early points of reference. . . . Every transference interpretation that successfully illuminates for the patient his unconscious past simultaneously crystallizes an illusive present—the novelty of the therapist as an understanding presence. Perceptions of self and other are perforce transformed and reshaped to allow for the new experience. Assimilation contributes the affective power inherent in the transference, while accommodation makes for change [Atwood and Stolorow, 1984, p. 60].

It should be clear from the foregoing passage that any attempt to separate the cognitive from the affective components of such structural transformations would be entirely artificial. The patient's insights into the nature of his unconscious organizing activity go hand in hand with new modes of affective bonding with the analyst, and both contribute to the patient's growing capacity to integrate conflictual, formerly dissociated experiential contents. As we have stressed throughout this book, sustained empathic inquiry into the patient's affective experiences of the analyst, and into the invariant principles that organize them, establish the therapeutic bond as an intersubjective context in which defensively sequestered and shackled regions of the patient's subjective life can be opened up and liberated.

When the selfobject dimension occupies the foreground of the transference, therapeutic action must be conceptualized not as a process of structural reorganization but of psychological structure *formation.* In our earlier (chapter 2) critique of Kohut's theory of optimal frustration leading to transmuting internalization, we suggested that structure formation occurs primarily when the selfobject dimension of the transference is intact or in the process of becoming restored. Innumerable selfobject experiences with the analyst provide a context that supports the development of the patient's capacity to assume a reflective, understanding, accepting, comforting attitude toward his own affective states and needs. (See Atwood and Stolorow, 1984, pp. 61–62, for an earlier discussion of this process.) Furthermore, the analyst's consistent acceptance and understanding of the patient's affective life come to be experienced by the patient as a facilitating medium reinstating arrested developmental processes of self-articulation and self-differentiation. Thus, the structuralization of self-experience is directly promoted by the stance of empathic inquiry. From this standpoint, as we have stated, the therapeutic benefit of analyzing ruptures in selfobject transference bonds lies in the integration of the disruptive affect states that such ruptures produce and in the concomitant mending and expanding of the broken selfobject tie. The selfobject dimension of the transference is seen as an archaic intersubjective matrix that, when intact or becoming mended, permits the patient's derailed psychological growth to resume. Once again we see that the cognitive and affective components of the therapeutic process cannot be separated, since it is the analyst's accurate interpretive activity that demonstrates his attunement to the patient's affective states and needs and that thereby makes it possible for the patient to establish the analytic bond as a source of requisite selfobject experiences.

CONCLUSION

Transference is conceptualized as a bipolar organization of experience, with continual oscillations in the figure-ground relationships between its selfobject and conflictual dimensions. These shifts occur in response to specific alterations in the intersubjective dialogue between analyst and patient. While the mode of therapeutic action of analysis depends on whether the selfobject or the conflictual dimension occupies the experiential foreground of the transference, in either case insight through interpretation, affective bonding through empathic attunement, and the facilitation of psychological integration are indissoluble facets of a unitary therapeutic process. Every interpretation derives its mutative power from the intersubjective system in which it takes form.

8

Treatment of Borderline States

The borderline concept has, in recent years, achieved enormous popularity within psychoanalytic and psychotherapeutic circles. Despite this rise to stardom, vast differences of opinion and numerous unresolved questions continue to exist concerning just what, if anything, the term "borderline" describes. We shall not attempt to cover the voluminous literature on this subject here (see Sugarman and Lerner, 1980, for an excellent review). Instead, we offer a critique of the currently prevalent view that the term "borderline" refers to a discrete pathological character structure, rooted in specific pathognomonic instinctual conflicts and primitive defenses. An alternative understanding of borderline phenomena emerges when they are viewed from an intersubjective perspective. Our focus will be on the intersubjective contexts in which borderline symptomatology takes form, both in early development and in the psychoanalytic situation.

The term "borderline" is generally used to refer to a distinct character structure that predisposes to faulty object relations, in which the fundamental difficulties are ordinarily attributed to the patient's pathological ego functioning. Typically the borderline personality organization is pictured as a direct structural consequence of the patient's use of certain primitive defenses—splitting, projective identification, idealization, and grandiosity—to ward off intense conflicts over dependency and excessive pregenital aggression (which dependency presumably mobilizes). But what is the clinical evidence that supposedly demonstrates the operation of these primitive defenses? And what is the meaning of the excessive aggression to which primary etiological significance is ascribed in the genesis of borderline psychopathology?

THE QUESTION OF SPLITTING

The experience of external objects as "all-good" or "all-bad" is generally regarded as a clear manifestation of splitting, resulting in sudden and total reversals of feeling whereby the view of the object is shifted from one extreme to the other. Oscillation between extreme and contradictory self concepts is similarly seen as evidence of splitting. This fluid and rapid alternation of contradictory perceptions of the self or others is seen as the result of an active defensive process whereby images with opposing affective valences are forcibly kept apart in order to prevent intense ambivalence. But is this assumption warranted clinically? Splitting as a defense actively employed to ward off ambivalence conflicts can come into play only after a minimum of integration of discrepant self and object experiences has been achieved through development (Stolorow and Lachmann, 1980). A defensive split into parts presupposes a prior integration of a whole. It is our contention that such a presupposition is not warranted when treating patients who are ordinarily diagnosed "borderline." Their fragmentary perceptions do not result primarily from defensive activity, but rather from an arrest in development, which impairs their ability reliably to synthesize affectively discrepant experiences of self and other. Their rapidly fluctuating views of the therapist, for example, do not primarily serve to prevent ambivalence toward him. They are, in part, manifestations of a need for the therapist to serve as an archaic containing or holding object whose consistently empathic *comprehension* and acceptance of these patients' contradictory affective states function as a facilitating medium through which their varying perceptions and feelings can eventually become better integrated (Winnicott, 1965; Modell, 1976; Stolorow and Lachmann, 1980).

It is our view that the lack of synthesis of self and object experiences characteristic of so-called borderline states is neither defensive in nature nor central in the genesis of these disorders. In our experience, the intense, contradictory affective states that these patients experience within the transference, and in particular their violent negative reactions, are indicative of specific structural weaknesses and vulnerabilities rooted in specific developmental interferences. Archaic mirroring, idealizing, and other selfobject needs are revived in analytic transferences, together with hopes for a resumption of development. When these needs are responded to, or understood and interpreted empathically, intense positive reactions occur. Similarly, when these needs are not recognized, responded to, or interpreted empathically, violent negative reactions may ensue. If these angry reactions are presumed to represent a defensive dissociation of good and bad aspects of objects, this in effect constitutes a covert demand that the patient ignore his own subjective experiences and appreciate the "goodness" of the analyst and his interpretations. It precludes analysis of the patient's subjective experience in depth, the elements that go to make it up, and their special hierarchy of meanings for the patient. In contrast, when we have held such preconceptions in abeyance, we have found that the intensity of the angry reactions stems from the way they encoded and encapsulated memories of specific traumatic childhood experiences.

The Case of Jeff

A clinical vignette illustrates our idea of a specific vulnerability. When Jeff, a young man of 23, entered treatment, he was in a state of marked overstimulation. He could not sit still for more than a few minutes at a time; his eyes darted from object to object; and he spoke under constant pressure. Although enrolled in college, he had not been able to attend classes or concentrate on his work. Increasingly frightened when alone at night, he had recently begun to take to the streets. There he had been approached for homosexual purposes several times, and this made him more fearful of his own unrecognized wishes and heightened his agitation. In the sessions he gave the impression of wanting desperately to cling to something around which he might begin to reorganize and restructure himself. Consequently, during the first months of treatment it was very difficult to bring any session to a close. His initial resistances centered on fears of being used to fulfill the analyst's needs. When these were interpreted, an early idealizing transference developed. This enabled Jeff to confront the area of primary defect—a failure to have attained a cohesive self and a vulnerability to recurrent states of protracted disorganization. The analysis thus resumed a developmental process that had been stalled.

Jeff's relationship with his father had always presented difficulty for him. The father reacted to any weakness or shortcoming in his son with impatience and contempt. This situation directly entered the analysis because Jeff's father had assumed financial responsibility for the treatment. The arrangement became a source of greater and greater tension between the two, for the father resented the burden of payment, as well as what he saw as evidence of his son's weakness and simultaneously a source of shame for himself. The difficulties in this area increased whenever Jeff made it clear that the analysis was not leading in the direction of making Jeff the son his father had always wished for, but was instead increasing Jeff's determination to develop in his own way.

Although the analyst realized the complications that might ensue, after two and a half years he notified Jeff that he was raising his fees generally. He wanted to discuss the matter with Jeff to see if and how it might be worked out. The request came at a time when Jeff's relations with his father were already strained, though it did not appear likely that this would change within any foreseeable period of time. Jeff's initial response was one of some anger about the unfortunate timing, followed by a remark to the effect that of course he knew how the analyst felt because everything was going up in price. Recognizing Jeff's frequent tendency to substitute an understanding of someone else's position for an expression of his own, the analyst interpreted this, together with Jeff's fear of the analyst's reaction to his expressing his own feeling. (We would emphasize that in our experience such genuine emotional expression is always obstructed, and with it an essential aspect of an authentic relationship, when a patient's affective states are incorrectly interpreted as defensive transference distortions.)

Gradually, over the course of the next few sessions, Jeff was able to come out with his feelings—feelings of hurt, disappointment, and violent anger. The hurt seemed to center on the analyst's failure to *ever* (Jeff's words) consider him first, and the extent to which this experience revived feelings of always having been a burden, a supplicant, someone standing in the way of other people's plans or enjoyment. Jeff was a twin, and he recounted a welter of experiences in which his twin had preempted his parents' attention by being exactly the child they wanted and one who caused them no difficulty.

Jeff's anger at the analyst was related mostly to the poor timing and what that meant to him. He spoke of the bind the analyst's request put him in. Things were already going badly between him and his father.

Jeff had started a new job and had been forced to ask his father for money for new clothes. Each encounter of that kind was humiliating for Jeff. Now he would have to face a review of how long he had been in treatment and how much longer it was to continue. How could the analyst, knowing all this, choose to put Jeff through it!

Frequently, after expressing himself unabashedly, Jeff would huddle up, as if in a corner, his arms protectively wrapped around himself. In response to questions, he confirmed that he was terrified. He was certain that the analyst would be furious with him, call him selfish, and berate him for his lack of appreciation for the analyst.

There now emerged a host of memories in which the timing of Jeff's life (and, indeed, his life itself) had to conform to someone else's wishes. He had to go to bed when his father told his mother he should. He had to wait until his father was done with the evening news before speaking to him, and then he could only talk about what his father was interested in. Monday night, football night, was especially sacrosanct—not an occasion when a pleasurable interest might be shared, but one more occasion when Dad was not to be disturbed.

Jeff's mother told him when, what, and how to eat. She chose his clothes for him, where and how he was to sit or stand. He was not to sit on the couch lest the cushions be messed up, nor on his bed for similar reasons. He had to renounce his own inclinations and adopt her wishes regarding what music he was to like. Always before the family left on an auto trip, he was instructed to urinate, and his mother checked to make sure he didn't put anything over on them. Otherwise they might have to stop along the way. And Jeff recalled that whenever he attempted to protest or assert himself, perhaps because something was especially important to him, he was squelched, accused of selfishness and a lack of consideration. He was told that his father wouldn't want to come home at all if he kept this up.

For Jeff, the most significant aspect of these repeated experiences was a feeling of absolute powerlessness. Once, when he could not stand it anymore, he went to his room and packed an overnight bag. When he appeared in front of his parents to declare he was running away, no one said a word or made a move to stop him. He then realized that he was stuck—that no one else would want him and that he had to give in.

These experiences formed the background of Jeff's reaction to the analyst's request for an increase. Jeff retained, in its most imperative form, the longing that someone would put his wishes first, and he was highly sensitive to the specific configuration of others' needs being put before his own. He therefore responded acutely and intensely to that configuration when it entered the transference. This response was covered over by a more moderate reaction, in which he apparently attempted defensively to "synthesize" good and bad object concepts. What was crucial, however, was for Jeff to recognize the underlying intensity of his hurt and the experiences behind it, rather than having his reaction regarded as an instance of splitting or a lack of appreciation for the analyst. This recognition opened up an entire area of the transference to analysis and ultimate resolution. Jeff and the analyst came to see clearly the extent to which Jeff had found it necessary to define himself around what was expected, what would please, and what would not offend in order to maintain his object ties. They were able to comprehend the threat constantly posed by any authentic experience of self—the threat of estrangement and isolation Jeff had encountered whenever he asserted himself or attempted to act on his own behalf. The analysis, then, brought out into the open and allowed Jeff to work through the enormous resentment such subjugation of self had aroused.

THE QUESTION OF PROJECTIVE IDENTIFICATION

Considerations similar to those we have discussed for splitting apply to the view of projective identification as a primitive defense, characteristic of borderline patients. In projective identification there is a blurring of the distinction between the self and the object in the area of the projected content. Such states of self-object confusion are presumed to be the product of an active defensive effort to externalize all-bad, aggressive self- and object images. Once again, we question whether this assumption is clinically justified.

Projection as a defense actively employed to ward off conflict can come into play only after a minimum of self-object differentiation has been reliably achieved (Stolorow and Lachmann, 1980). Defensive translocation of mental content across self-object boundaries presupposes that those boundaries have been for the most part consolidated. Our experience contradicts such a presupposition for patients diagnosed "borderline." Their states of self-object confusion arise primarily from a developmentally determined inability to maintain the distinction between self and object. In the treatment context it is not useful to view such states as examples of either defensive projection or general ego weakness. Instead, these partially undifferentiated states are best understood as manifestations of revivals with the therapist of a specific need for immersion in a nexus of archaic relatedness, from within which formerly thwarted developmental processes of self-articulation and self-demarcation can be revitalized and once again resumed (Stolorow and Lachmann, 1980).

Frequently we have encountered in the literature a second, and to our minds even more questionable, use of the term "projective identification." There is presumed to be not only a projective distortion of the patient's subjective experience of the object, but also a purposefully induced alteration in the external object's actual attitude and behavior toward the patient. The patient is said to put split-off, disavowed parts of himself inside the external object. This formulation is based on the observation that intense reactions frequently occur in analysts who are treating borderline patients. Because such reactions are experienced similarly by most "reasonably well-adjusted therapists," the reasoning goes, "countertransference reactions in these cases reflect the patient's problems much more than any specific problems of the analyst's past" (Kernberg, 1975, p. 54). It is also suggested that if the analyst is reacting intensely to the patient, such countertransference is a clue to the patient's hidden intention. Kernberg (1975), for example, writes:

> If the patient systematically rejects all the analyst's interpretations over a long period of time, the analyst may recognize his own resultant feelings of impotence and point out to the patient that he is treating the analyst as if he wished to make him feel defeated and impotent. Or when antisocial behavior in the patient makes the analyst, rather than the patient, worry about the consequences, the analyst may point out that the patient seems to try to let the analyst feel the concern over his behavior because the patient himself cannot tolerate such a feeling [p. 247].

These formulations fail to take into account that when the analyst, in his interpretations, insists that the patient's difficulties arise from vicissitudes of aggressive-drive processing, the only alternatives open to the patient are to agree with the premises being put forward or to find himself in the position of *inadvertently* making the analyst feel defeated and impotent. To us, this state of affairs seems to reflect the extent to which the analyst's self-esteem depends on the patient's acceptance of the correctness of his theoretical position, rather than necessarily reflecting any unconscious hostile intention on the part of the patient. Similarly, the analyst's concerns about a patient's antisocial behavior seem to us to reflect the analyst's difficulties in sufficiently demarcating himself from the patient so as to be able to devote himself to the investigation of the meaning of the actions in question.

A description of a typical clinical application of the concept of projective identification is contained in Kernberg's (1975) reference to Ingmar Bergman's movie *Persona*:

> A recent motion picture . . . illustrates the breakdown of an immature but basically decent young woman, a nurse, charged with the care of a psychologically severely ill woman presenting what we would describe as a typical narcissistic personality. In the face of the cold, unscrupulous exploitation to which the young nurse is subjected she gradually breaks down. She cannot face the fact that the other sick woman returns only hatred for love and is completely unable to acknowledge any loving or human feeling toward her. The sick woman seems able to live only if and when she can destroy what is valuable in other persons, although in the process she ends up by destroying herself as a human being. In a dramatic development the nurse develops an intense hatred for the sick woman and mistreats her cruelly at one point. It is as if all the hatred within the sick woman had been transferred into the helpful one, destroying the helping person from the inside [pp. 245–246].

We hold that conclusions such as this are unjustified and that the underlying assumptions are unwarranted and antitherapeutic. In the first place, there is no evidence that the sick woman is "able to live only if and when she can destroy what is valuable in other persons"; there are only indications that the sick woman does not respond in a way that the nurse-therapist wants or needs. We are familiar in our own practices with many cases in which patients who have recently experienced traumatic loss and disintegration resolutely protect themselves against any involvement until some spontaneous recovery has set in. Second, there is no evidence that "the hatred within the sick woman has been transferred into the helpful one, destroying the helping person from the inside." There is, instead, every indication that the patient's responsiveness was required in order for the nurse to maintain her own self-esteem and to regulate her own psychological functioning. When frustrated, the nurse demonstrated her own narcissistic vulnerability and propensity for rage reactions. We have observed such factors at work in ourselves and regard them as to some degree universal in therapeutic relationships. In our view, their near universality does not warrant their being ignored as originating in the personality structure of the therapist. Nor does it warrant the assumption that these responses are an indication of pathological projective mechanisms on the part of the patient. We have found that the assumption that the patient wishes the therapist to feel impotent or infuriated is much more often than not directly contradicted in our own work. Such wishes, we suggest, occur only when the patient's disagreements, assertions, and primary wishes to have his own subjective experiences empathically understood have been consistently unresponded to. Far more often, the patient's fear of the analyst's narcissistic vulnerability and of being held responsible for the analyst's feeling of frustration constitutes a severe resistance to free association and is a prominent motive for defense.

The concept of projective identification is used extensively by analysts to explain any fear that is not readily intelligible as a response to a real danger. It is consistently invoked to explain why patients are so regularly afraid of their analysts. We have found, however, that the analyst's insistence that negative reactions in analysis are to be explained by the patient's innate aggression or envy, or by his projection of aggressively distorted internal objects, can be damaging to the patient, to the unfolding selfobject transference, and to the analysis (Brandchaft, 1983).

The application of the theory of projective identification carries with it the real danger of depriving patients of a means of defending themselves when they feel that the analyst is cruel, distant, controlling, or demeaning. This danger is increased if the analyst, for whatever reason, is unable or unwilling to become aware of his actual effect on the patient, or if he minimizes that effect because of a conviction that he has the ultimate best interests of the patient at heart. Frequently, this conviction in the analyst takes the form of a conception of a "more normal dependent" part of the patient, which is being dominated and excluded by the aggressive part. Such unwarranted, if reassuring, concepts notwithstanding, the tendency to fall back on interpretations of projection to the detriment of the subjective experience of the patient, even where such mechanisms exist, can in practice be shown to foster a dependence on the analyst's perceptions at the expense of the patient's. These interpretations encourage, indeed require, a *pro forma* belief in the analyst's "goodness" and correctness at the expense of the self. They impair the patient's sense of his own self and belief in himself, and they encourage an agreement that necessary and understandable efforts to protect a vulnerable self are indicative of severe pathology and should be given up.

FURTHER MISCONCEPTUALIZATIONS

Closely allied with the developmental disturbances discussed so far are the idealizations and grandiosity that often pervade the treatment of patients who are called "borderline." Such perceptions of the self or others are regularly interpreted as being defensive against dependency and the attendant subject-centered or object-centered aggression. Our experiences indicate that most often the idealizations and grandiosity are manifestations of selfobject transferences (Kohut, 1971, 1977). They are not pathological defenses, but rather revivals with the therapist of the archaic idealizing and mirroring ties that were traumatically and phase-inappropriately ruptured during the patient's formative years and on which he now comes to rely for the restoration and maintenance of his sense of self and for the resumption and completion of his arrested psychological growth.

Having argued that much of the clinical evidence cited for the operation of primitive defenses is actually evidence of needs for specific archaic selfobject ties, and of disturbances in those ties, how shall we understand the "excessive pregenital aggression" that many authors believe is the etiological bedrock of borderline pathology? We contend that pervasive primitive aggression is an inevitable, unwitting, iatrogenic consequence of a therapeutic approach that presupposes that the psychological configurations we have been discussing are in their essence pathological defenses against dependency and primitive aggression. A patient revives an arrested archaic state or need, or attempts a previously aborted developmental step within the therapeutic relationship, and the therapist interprets this developmental necessity as if it were a pathological defense. The patient then experiences this misinterpretation as a gross failure of attunement, a severe breach of trust, a traumatic narcissistic wound (Stolorow and Lachmann, 1980). When vital developmental requirements reexperienced in relation to the therapist once again meet with traumatically unempathic responses, is it surprising that such misunderstandings often bring intense rage and destructiveness in their wake? We are contending, in other words, that the pervasive aggression is not etiological, but rather a secondary reaction to the therapist's inability to comprehend the developmental meaning of the patient's archaic states and of the archaic bond that the patient needs to establish with him (Kohut, 1972, 1977; Stolorow, 1984a).

AN INTERSUBJECTIVE VIEWPOINT

At this point we are in a position to formulate our central thesis regarding the borderline concept. The psychological essence of what we call "borderline" is *not* that it is a pathological condition located solely in the patient. Rather, *it refers to phenomena arising in an intersubjective field—a field consisting of a precarious, vulnerable self in a failing, archaic selfobject bond.* In order to elaborate this thesis further, we must clarify the nature of the self disorder that contributes to the emergence of borderline phenomena.

We view the various disorders of the self as arbitrary points along a continuum (see Adler, 1981) rather than as discrete diagnostic entities. The points along this continuum are defined by the degree of impairment and vulnerability of the sense of self, the acuteness of the threat of its disintegration, and the motivational urgency of self-reparative efforts in various pathological states. The degree of severity of self disorder may be evaluated with reference to three essential features of the sense of self—its structural cohesion, temporal stability, and affective coloration (Stolorow and Lachmann, 1980).

In certain patients, the sense of self is negatively colored (feelings of low self-esteem) but is for the most part temporally stable and structurally cohesive. One might refer to such cases as mild self disorders. In other patients, the sense of self is negatively colored *and* its organization is temporally unstable (experiences of identity confusion) but, notwithstanding fleeting fragmentations, it largely retains its structural cohesion. These cases might be called moderately severe self disorders. In a third group of patients, the sense of self is negatively colored, temporally unstable, *and* lacking in cohesion and thus subject to protracted structural fragmentation and disintegration. Such cases can be termed very severe self disorders. Roughly speaking, patients who are called "borderline" fall within the moderate to severe range of self disorders.

Our concept of self disorder as a continuum or dimension of psychopathology is somewhat at variance with Kohut's (1971) early view of "borderline" as a discrete diagnostic entity that is sharply distinguishable from the narcissistic personality disorders. The borderline personality, according to this view, is chronically threatened with the possibility of an irreversible disintegration of the self—a psychological catastrophe that is more or less successfully averted by the various protective operations characteristic of borderline functioning. This vulnerability to a permanent breakup of the self is the product of a traumatically crushing or depriving developmental history that has precluded even minimal consolidation of the archaic grandiose self and the idealized parent imago. Consequently, unlike the narcissistic personality, the borderline patient is unable to form a stable mirroring or idealizing selfobject transference and is therefore unanalyzable by the classical method.

In contrast with Kohut's conceptualization, our observations are consistent with those of other analysts who have reported analyses of borderline personalities in which the therapist *was* eventually able to help the patient form a more or less stable and analyzable selfobject transference (Adler, 1980, 1981; Tolpin, 1980). It is true that the selfobject ties formed by those patients who are called "borderline" tend initially to be far more primitive and intense, more labile and vulnerable to disruption, and therefore more taxing of the therapist's empathy and tolerance (Adler, 1980, 1981; Tolpin, 1980) than those described by Kohut as being characteristic of narcissistic personalities. Furthermore, when the selfobject ties of a patient with a moderate to severe self disorder are obstructed or ruptured by misunderstandings or separations, the patient's reactions may be much more catastrophic and disturbed, for what is threatened is the patient's central self-regulatory capacity—the basic structural integrity and stability of the sense of self, not merely its affective tone (Adler, 1980, 1981; Stolorow and Lachmann, 1980). Nevertheless, when their archaic states and needs are sufficiently understood, these patients can be helped to form more or less stable selfobject transferences, and, when this is achieved, their so-called borderline features recede and even disappear. As long as the selfobject tie to the therapist remains intact, their treatment will bear a close similarity to Kohut's descriptions of analyses of narcissistic personality disorders (Adler, 1980, 1981).[1] When the selfobject tie to the therapist becomes significantly disrupted, on the other hand, the patient may once again present borderline features. What we wish to stress is that whether or not a stable selfobject bond can develop and be maintained (which in turn shapes both the apparent diagnostic picture and the assessment of analyzability) does not depend only on the patient's nuclear self pathology. It will be codetermined by the extent of the therapist's ability to comprehend the nature of the patient's archaic subjective universe (Tolpin, 1980) as it begins to structure the microcosm of the therapeutic transference.

The Case of Caroline

Our conception of borderline as phenomena arising and receding within an intersubjective field is exemplified by the case of Caroline. The "borderline" symptoms that led Caroline to enter analysis were immediately precipitated by severe disturbances in her relationship with her husband. In other words, they arose within a specific intersubjective field—that of a precarious, vulnerable self in a failing, archaic selfobject tie. The analyst, however, did not sufficiently recognize this when the treatment began, and his lack of understanding complicated and prolonged the treatment. We have since observed that most often patients enter treatment when there is a breakdown in an archaic selfobject bond, which has hitherto served to maintain, however precariously and at whatever cost, the structural cohesion and stability of the self and the patient's central self-regulatory capability.

[1]In a personal communication (1981), Kohut stated that he had long held views compatible with those developed here. He wrote: "Insofar as the therapist is able to build an empathic bridge to the patient, the patient has in a way ceased to be a borderline case . . . and has become a case of [severe] narcissistic personality disorder."

Caroline's two previous attempts at treatment had not materially affected the underlying defect in her self-structure. When she entered the analysis described here, she was 42 years old. Her last analysis had ended about three years earlier when her analyst told her he didn't feel he could do any more for her. Since that time she had thrown herself into various pursuits. She had returned to school to finish her education, which had been interrupted many years before when she married. In addition, she had involved herself in some charitable and social activities in an attempt "to feel useful" and to keep herself occupied.

Caroline spoke with a Southern accent, which became more pronounced when she was tense. She was somewhat overweight and attempted to cover this with loose-fitting clothes, which only made it stand out more. For some time she had been in a state of more or less constant anxiety, at times hyperactive and at other times withdrawn, apathetic, and unable to get moving. Early in her treatment, she displayed a frightened, little-girl look, expressing her evident discomfort and not infrequently her terror. She avoided the analyst's eyes almost completely. In the first weeks, she openly voiced her disbelief that anyone could help her and said she saw no way out of her difficulties.

Gradually it was reconstructed that her present intractable state dated from about 10 years earlier and had followed a deterioration in her relationship with her husband (to whom she had then been married for about a dozen years). Although Caroline had been a reasonably attractive young woman, her shyness and lack of confidence, in concert with a puritanical upbringing, had constricted her social and sexual development. Thus, her husband was the first man with whom she had had a serious relationship. She had been an outstanding student—her remarkable intelligence was to become clearer as the treatment progressed—but she left college when she married, in order to support and further the career of her husband, then in law school. Subsequently, when he set up practice, she kept house for him, assisted him in many ways, reared their child, and operated a small business so that they could prosper financially. In spite of this, their relationship became more strained and conflicted, as her husband became ever more displeased with and critical of her—of her accent, her weight, her anxiety and depression. This culminated in a "borderline" state, with progressive lethargy, hypochondriacal symptoms, feelings of deadness that began in her extremities and threatened to engulf her whole body, and frightening delusions about her husband harming, poisoning, or killing her.

Caroline recovered from this early episode in a matter of weeks, but many of the symptoms recurred (though not the delusions) and other symptoms took hold. She began to eat compulsively, and there were periodic withdrawals during which she remained preoccupied with puzzles or needlework for long periods of time. In the early months of treatment, Caroline appeared so distraught and disorganized that the analyst believed that only by seeing her six times a week could he avert a prolonged hospitalization or suicide (to which she made several references).

Whatever the content of the sessions, Caroline reacted to their ending with enormous anxiety and clung to the analyst as the hour drew to a close, speeding up her associations so that he could not interrupt her. When he succeeded in calling the session to a halt, she either continued the conversation until he closed the door behind her or, enraged by his interrupting her, walked out in a sullen pout. Weekends and more prolonged separations produced severe regressive states and numerous dreams filled with disaster—flooding and drowning, houses perched precariously on a cliff edge, supports crumbling, black men pursuing her, and imagery involving a variety of mutilations.

In the first dream that Caroline reported in the analysis, she described her husband and her analyst sitting in the living room. She went to the freezer and took something out. It was the trunk of a frozen corpse with no limbs. She showed this to the men, but they began to have sport with it—tossing it around and laughing.

The early sessions were marked by an almost uninterrupted stream of associations. The analyst found it hard to think, let alone formulate a coherent understanding of any underlying meaning. As this continued for some time, it was difficult for the analyst to escape the conviction that she was projecting her anxiety and helplessness into him in an attempt to rid herself of these feelings.

Gradually, however, it became clear that she was terrified of the analyst and the treatment—terrified that she would be treated cruelly, driven mad, or abandoned as a hopeless case. These fears were interpreted to her as indications of a lack of trust and reluctance to depend on the analyst. Such interpretations seemed for a time to calm her, and they evoked memories of her early experiences.

Caroline was the first child of her mother and father. They had married when her mother was approaching 40. Her father, four years older and a widower with two teen-aged sons, was a hard-working accountant who needed someone to take responsibility for their upbringing. As a young woman, Caroline's mother had wanted desperately to escape from the drudgery of her small town life, and her love of music seemed to offer her the opportunity. But she realized rather late that her hopes of becoming an opera singer or the coach of an operatic prodigy were destined to disappointment. By that time her chances for a good marriage had passed her by, and she settled on Caroline's father, more with resignation than ardor, a bird in no gilded cage.

Caroline was born two years later, after what she was repeatedly told was an extremely difficult labor. Three years after her birth a brother was born. This birth was even more difficult and resulted in severe damage to the mother's pelvic tissues. Afterward the mother took to her bed in a depression that lasted for many months during which time she was preoccupied with an assortment of hypochondriacal and somatic symptoms. When she recovered, she treated Caroline as if the little girl were an extension of her own defective, diseased self. She reacted to every sneeze as if it were a harbinger of death, took Caroline from doctor to doctor, and kept her out of school for two years. As Caroline and her health became her mother's sole preoccupation, intense conflicts arose. These centered on what foods Caroline was to eat, how much and at what intervals she was to sleep, and especially her bowel habits.

As the treatment progressed, the analyst noted that Caroline was somewhat better as each week proceeded, but then regressed toward its end. Weekends remained disasters, with the patient unable to think or function except at a minimal level. The analyst thought that the material indicated Caroline's inability to retain any image of a good object built up during the sessions—she and it underwent a nearly complete deterioration during separations. When she returned to analysis, it was in a state of helplessness. Repeatedly, she then complained that the analysis was not helping her, and frequently, apparently forgetting her condition when she entered treatment, she angrily asserted that the analyst was responsible for her pain and lack of progress.

It was easy for the analyst to conclude that the archaic states of confusion and disintegration into which Caroline lapsed came about because of persistent splitting, that her good internal objects were being kept widely apart from the bad, that synthesis was being actively prevented from occurring, and that she could not simultaneously accept the analyst's goodness and his separateness. She reacted to his unavailability on weekends and to what he believed were thoughtful and helpful interpretations as if they were purposely meant to make her suffer. Attacking him in that way, she anticipated being attacked in return. And she experienced every attempt on his part to explain this situation to her, no matter how cautiously, tactfully, and empathically phrased, as a renewed attack on her.

Another "symptom" appeared in Caroline's treatment. One day, in striking contrast to her usual outfit of jeans and tennis shoes, she appeared in a lovely skirt and jacket, a pretty blouse, and fashionable shoes and purse. Greatly embarrassed, she revealed that she had gone on a spree, bought three outfits, several pairs of shoes, and an assortment of matching accessories. She confided that she did this every once in a while, in spite of herself. She knew that when she went home she would have to hide all the things she had bought and might never be able to wear them, for her husband would be furious with her. He would be frightened and horrified by her excesses. He maintained absolute control over the family finances and regarded her buying binges as symptoms of insanity or as inconsiderate breaches of contract. Moreover, now he would have further grounds for his understandable concern over her treatment.

The analyst felt that if her purpose was to project into him her anxiety over behavior for which she wished to escape responsibility, she could not have devised a more effective means. He was also struck by the excess, the suddenness, and the lack of control, and he tried, without success, to investigate the spree from that perspective. He was to learn later that Caroline did not buy another stitch of clothing for three years.

Caroline's fears of the analyst and the analysis kept recurring. Her dreams were filled with scalding suns, Chinese tortures, and monstrously cruel people. Such images were generally interpreted as transference projections. And gradually some small progress seemed to occur. Her anger subsided somewhat, her anxiety assumed more manageable proportions, and she was able to read and to socialize to a greater extent. Yet whenever her old symptoms returned, she thrashed herself mercilessly. Repeated working through of these themes seemed to the analyst to leave no alternative to the explanation that something in her was opposing success, making it impossible for her to benefit further from treatment, her marriage, and, indeed, her life. She made many starts in many directions, but invariably her enthusiasm disappeared, to be mourned and to become the focus of renewed disappointment and anger with herself. It seemed that continued treatment would only confirm an omnipotent fantasy that somehow some experience would magically solve her difficulties without her having to change.

The analysis, then, appeared to have reached a stalemate. Although basic problems had not been solved, the prospect of termination loomed unmistakably, for it seemed to the analyst that more analysis would only serve to keep Caroline from utilizing the considerable insights she had attained. Rationalizations appeared like weeds after a rain. After all, her background had left her with a considerable toll. The difficulties of her attachment to or detachment from her husband, especially at her age, were all but insurmountable. Her gains, looked at in a certain light, were not negligible, and it seemed certain that she was no longer so vulnerable to the threat of collapse that had brought her into treatment.

In the fourth year of treatment, with many of Caroline's borderline features still intact, the analyst decided to take one last look. It had long been apparent that Caroline was disappointed and felt herself to be a failure, but it was now also becoming clear that she felt that the *analyst* was disappointed in her and that *he* considered her and himself failures. This factor—Caroline's responsiveness to cues of the analyst's feeling about her—had been grossly underestimated. In fact, as was later understood, her imperative need to be liked and approved of and the devastating effect on her of the analyst's disapproval, which she sensed, had been crucial in structuring the first phase of treatment. Her depression, her attacks on herself, and her lack of sustaining motivation all became understandable from this perspective. The analyst could not continue to maintain that her perceptions of him were all projection, for he began to recognize in himself what she had been responding to. This dawning awareness ushered in the second phase of the analysis.

In a subsequent session, in response to Caroline's expression of weariness and thoughts about terminating, the analyst commented that he realized that the process was becoming wearing. But could they take one more good look at what had been occurring before deciding to terminate? Perhaps there was something he had not understood, something that might prove helpful. Perhaps he had conveyed an increasing disappointment in her and in himself, especially around her continuing symptoms, and perhaps that had contributed in an important way to her dejection and disparagement of herself. Caroline responded enthusiastically. Yes, she exclaimed, she had felt awful about the analyst's disappointment, which she had sensed. By this time she should be able to feel better and to control her diet, for she had learned so much. She had attacked herself mercilessly for not having tried hard enough. She was weak and self-indulgent, she said, and must want to spite both her husband and the analyst as she had always defied her mother. When she was on her diets, she could somehow kill her craving for food and not be hungry. But something always happened and she again felt the urge to eat. Then she felt she was a failure and tried harder and harder. When she was finally unable to stick to her diet, she hated herself, for she had let the analyst and her husband down. *Once that point had been reached she was absolutely unable to restrain herself—the more alone she felt, the more she hated herself and the more she felt compelled to eat.*

The analyst was now able to glimpse the transference configuration that had actually determined the course of Caroline's analysis. Together they began to look at what happened to her when she was alone, paying increasing attention now to her subjective experiences and trying to understand them in a different way. There seemed to be a complex and thoroughgoing alteration of her state of mind—a slipping away of self-esteem, feelings of accelerating disorganization and disconnectedness, an inability to concentrate, and increasing feelings of deadness, involving coldness and loss of sensation in her limbs, so that they no longer seemed to belong to her. All these symptoms the analyst came to recognize as signs of a fragmenting process and of an underlying defect in her self-structure. It became apparent how much Caroline had looked to the analyst to maintain her sense of self, needing from him what had not been acquired in her childhood. When the analyst had interpreted her archaic states and transference needs as expressions of pathological splitting and projection, she had become intensely ashamed and self-hating. In their impact on Caroline, the interpretations of pathological defenses had repeated the fragmentation-producing effects of her mother's view of her as defective and diseased.

It was especially important to Caroline that the analyst be pleased with her. She had tried valiantly to get this across to him early in the analysis, but he had regarded this as defensive. He had not recognized as primary her specific need to establish him as a selfobject who would be a source of the mirroring, affirming responsiveness that her self-absorbed, depressed, and hypochondriacal mother had been unable to supply during her early formative years. Behind this specific need lay the vulnerability to fragmentation that had pervaded Caroline's analytic experiences. When the selfobject tie to the analyst was disrupted by a failure of the analyst to understand her subjective experience in its essence or by a loss of connectedness during weekends or vacations, she could not maintain the cohesion, stability, and affective tone of her precarious self. She fell apart, eating compulsively in an effort to strengthen herself and to fill the defect in her sense of self—trying to recover through oral self-stimulation the feeling that she existed at all.

As the structural weakness was being worked through, Caroline realized at one point that she was becoming addicted to television and radio. When she thought about the vague, apprehensive restlessness she felt in the absence of sensory stimulation, she realized that "empty" did not really describe her feeling. Rather, she recognized "a feeling of deficiency, a lack of some very specific supporting structure which would prevent everything from falling in—some essential piece of myself missing." When the analyst had taken her symptoms as a disparagement of his efforts, as a defensive aggrandizement of herself, or as an indication of greed, she had felt even worse. Feeling blamed, she had relentlessly blamed herself.

As the disturbance in the transference tie was seen and analyzed in this new way, with focus on the fragmented states and the underlying structural deficit, Caroline became more alive, friendlier, much more enthusiastic, and increasingly capable. Her desire to understand her states of mind grew in direct proportion to her sense of the analyst's desire to help her acquire this understanding. She expressed appreciation that the analyst now recognized her vulnerability and the legitimacy of her fears. "The first thing I had to get across to you," she explained when she was certain that he would understand her, "was how important what you thought of me was. Until that happened nothing else could happen. I couldn't disagree with you because I was afraid of worse consequences. So I tried to see and use and apply what you said, even when it made me hate myself. I tried to think you were opening up a new world for me, a new way of seeing things that would work out better in the end. And when it wasn't working out that way, I blamed myself."

With the working through of her fragmented states in relation to their triggering experiences within a disrupted selfobject tie, Caroline's borderline symptomatology and paranoidlike fears dropped away, together with what had previously been regarded as splitting, projection, and a failure to internalize a good object. She and the analyst could now better understand her dream of the frozen torso and her expectations of being laughed at. She had often been terrified as a little girl, but her fears had always been mocked. She could not, for example, let her mother bathe her or wash her hair, and her mother would be furious with her. No one understood why she was afraid of her mother—indeed, afraid of almost everything. She was teased mercilessly by her brothers for being so afraid. "Girls can't do anything," they would say.

As Caroline's vulnerability decreased, there were increasing signs that she was turning once more to the analyst to help her understand her early relationship with her mother, its effect on her, and how crucial elements were being replicated with her husband and the analyst. The analyst could now understand the symbolism of an earlier turning, which he had missed. Her buying binge had contained both her fear and her intense need to be noticed. As a girl, she had turned to her father to be noticed, for it was only through connecting herself to him that she felt she might be able to extricate herself from the traumatogenic enmeshment with her mother. "But he was remote and embarrassed by emotion—even by mother's emotion, and even though he loved mother," she remarked. "When feelings were expressed, he would look away. Then, after a point, he would introduce another subject, as if what had taken place before did not exist." Caroline remembered wanting her father to pick her up, but he never did, except as part of a game. She didn't play right, she felt, so she couldn't be held. And she so wanted him to want to be close to her. She realized now that when the analyst spoke to her gently and smiled when he greeted her, she felt real and warm, not frozen. If she had been feeling bad and hating herself, that made her feel all right.

Caroline had blamed herself when her father hadn't noticed her or loved her. In particular, she had blamed her anger. The anger evoked by her father's unresponsiveness had been enormously threatening to her because of her desperate need for him. Thus, she exonerated him and blamed her reactive anger for his faulty responsiveness. A similar sequence could be observed in reaction to unattuned responses from her husband and the analyst. Her idealizations were not primarily a defense against her anger. Rather, she preserved the vitally needed idealizations *at the expense* of her anger and of her ability to assert herself when her interests were disregarded.

Caroline had turned to her father not primarily as an oedipal love object, but as an idealized selfobject whose responsive interest in her might open a compensatory path along which her thwarted development could resume. When this developmental thrust was revived in the transference, her associations led her back to her fourth and fifth years. Her memories clearly showed that what she most needed her father to notice and understand was what she was going through with her mother. In the analysis she realized that she had to return to that time because something had happened then that had made her life thereafter almost unbearable. She remembered herself before this time as a well-dressed little girl; afterward she felt like a ragamuffin.

When Caroline was four her mother, then recovering from a prolonged depression, had resumed her involvement with the church as an organist and choral leader. The church and the little girl largely made up the boundaries of the mother's restricted world. Even then her mother would often go to bed for the day, saying, "I know I can't get out today." Caroline remembered that during this period she had wanted to learn to play the piano. Taking affront that Caroline might want anyone else to teach her, her mother undertook the task. Caroline recalled that as with everything else, her mother insisted on a strict routine—first, months of finger exercises away from the piano, and only then the real thing. Her mother was an overwhelming teacher. When Caroline tried and pleaded, "I can't," her mother flew into a rage. Later, Caroline came to understand that the rage was toward her mother's own recalcitrant self, indistinguishable from that of her daughter. The mother desperately wished that her daughter would not give up, as she herself had done, that Caroline would not become a nobody doing the things in the kitchen no one else wanted to do. She insisted that Caroline did not care about her, did not value her. Caroline could see that her mother believed this, and it scared her. But then she told herself perhaps her mother was right, perhaps she would never be able to care for anyone (as she was also told) if she couldn't care for her mother. It was so frightening to think that her mother didn't understand her that she found it a relief to believe that she herself was bad.

Why couldn't she practice, her mother would ask. It was just a matter of moving her fingers. Her mother would demonstrate and then take Caroline's fingers and show her. It could only be rebelliousness, Caroline was always so stubborn. Then her mother would get out the whip as the little girl froze and cowered. It was a black, braided leather affair with a number of thongs, perfect equipment for not spoiling the child. Although it was only used three or four times, Caroline would remember her fear and humiliation for the rest of her life. That ended her career in music.

One of the most terrifying aspects of these childhood experiences was that something was glaringly wrong, but nobody seemed to know it or do anything about it. When Caroline went to her father, he would change the subject. When she went to the maid, she was told how it was to be an orphan as the maid had been. Caroline had to find some way to live with her mother, so she made herself responsible, telling herself that if she were better her mother would love her. "It is terrifying to be in the power of another person," she observed. The feeling that something was wrong and nobody seemed to know or do anything about it was replicated in the analysis when the analyst failed to respond to Caroline's assertions of the threat to herself posed by many of his interpretations.

There was something even worse than whipping, Caroline realized one day. One of the major methods by which her mother controlled her was by continuously threatening to leave her. That was always, and still remained, the ultimate whip, both with her husband and in the transference. *She realized that the threat may have been completely false objectively, but it was very real to her.* Even now, anyone she needed could reduce her to submission by threatening to leave her. Her mother had simply walked away from her when the little girl had "misbehaved" or acted cranky. "It is almost as if you have a choice of existing or your mother existing, but not both," Caroline explained. The meaning of a remark at the beginning of the analysis was now more understandable: "I have had to be able to hate my mother in order to stay alive!"

Caroline recalled that the family had a small house near the ocean, at the mouth of a river. Her mother was afraid Caroline would drown and so insisted on teaching her to swim—not in the small river but in the ocean. Yet her mother herself could barely swim. Caroline remembered her terror when her mother approached her. She couldn't let her mother near her! She couldn't tolerate looking at her because she knew that just the touch or the look would immediately cause her to lose herself, not feel herself. Her mother frequently said, "If you could just see yourself through somebody else's eyes." Caroline realized how much she had needed for someone to see through her eyes. In the water she would scream, "I'll do it myself; please let me do it myself!" Her mother would stand over her, coldly retorting, "When are you going to do it? When are you going to do it?"

Caroline often imagined running away from her mother's ruthless training. One day, in the analysis, she spoke of this, remarking, "If I had had a father to run to, I would have." It was when she saw all her little friends playing and going places with their fathers that she began to feel like a ragamuffin. She remembered so much wanting to run away, but she was concerned about not having any food. She began to think about packing food in small packages. She collected Tarzan books, and she recalled being fascinated because he was able to survive in the jungle with only a knife; he didn't have to depend on or submit to anyone. Eventually, however, her daydreams of escaping from her mother collapsed. She was too aware of reality and knew that she would have to come back, so she made her peace.

At this stage of the analysis, Caroline remarked on a feeling of being better integrated. The analyst had allowed her to revive in the transference the longed-for selfobject bond to an idealized father, who would help her understand and separate from her pathological enmeshment with her mother. Everything she thought about now seemed more vivid, she commented. Her thoughts and feelings made more sense to her. She felt more self-confidence, although she was still worried that this would disappear and not return. Still, she felt she was stronger, as she put it, than the threat to her was. Moreover, she noted an increased ability to stick to her moderated diet. Slowly but noticeably, she began to lose weight. There was much more to be done, she realized, but she felt that a corner had been turned, as indeed it had.

To summarize this case: Caroline's adult "borderline" characteristics and paranoidlike distrust had arisen in the intersubjective field of her vulnerable, fragmentation-prone self within a failing, archaic selfobject tie (with her husband). These borderline characteristics remained and were periodically intensified in the new intersubjective field of the psychoanalytic situation when the analyst's incorrect interpretive stance and faulty responsiveness unwittingly triggered and exacerbated her states of self-fragmentation. The failures in her marital relationship and in the first phase of the analysis replicated the specific, traumatogenic selfobject failures of her early childhood years. Caroline had adapted to these failures by attempting to serve the archaic selfobject needs of her mother and pushing herself even harder when her mother found her wanting in that role. This was repeated with the analyst. In contrast, in the second phase of the analysis, when the analyst became able to comprehend the actual meaning of Caroline's archaic subjective states and needs, thereby permitting her to revive and establish with him the specific selfobject ties that she required, her so-called borderline features dropped away.

CONCLUSION

We have criticized the view that the term "borderline" designates a distinct pathological character structure, rooted in pathognomonic instinctual conflicts and primitive defenses. Instead, we propose an alternative conceptualization of so-called borderline phenomena from an intersubjective perspective. In particular, we believe that the clinical evidence cited for the operation of primitive defenses against pregenital aggression is better understood as an indication of needs for specific archaic selfobject ties, and of disturbances in those ties. As the case of Caroline suggests, the psychological essence of what is called "borderline" does not rest in a pathological condition located solely in the patient. Rather, it lies in phenomena arising in an intersubjective field, consisting of a precarious, vulnerable self in a failing, archaic selfobject bond.

We wish to clarify some potential sources of misunderstanding of our point of view. Conceptualizing borderline phenomena as arising in an intersubjective field is *not* equivalent to claiming that the term "borderline" refers to an entirely iatrogenic illness. As seen in the case of Caroline, the failing, archaic selfobject bond is not always with a therapist or an analyst, although this will become increasingly more likely as the patient's selfobject needs are engaged in the therapeutic transference. More importantly, the claim of an entirely iatrogenic illness would be markedly at variance with our concept of an *intersubjective* field and would overlook the contribution of the patient's archaic states, arrested needs, and fragmentation-prone self to the formation of that psychological field. If we view the therapeutic situation as an intersubjective field, then we must see that the patient's manifest psychopathology is always *codetermined* by the patient's self disorder *and* the therapist's ability to understand it.

Our claim is not that borderline symptomatology is entirely iatrogenic, but that the *concept* of a "borderline personality organization" is largely, if not entirely, an iatrogenic myth. We believe that the idea of a borderline character structure rooted in pathognomonic conflicts and defenses is symptomatic of the difficulty therapists have had in comprehending the archaic intersubjective contexts in which borderline pathology arises.

We wish to emphasize that selfobject failures are developmentally codetermined subjective experiences of the patient and that therefore their occurrence in treatment is not to be regarded as an objective index of the therapist's technical incompetence or inadequacy. They are revivals in the transference of the patient's early history of developmental deprivation and interference. Thus, the therapeutic task is not to avert such experiences of selfobject failure but to *analyze* them from within the unique perspective of the patient's subjective world.

From the standpoint of the archaic nature of the arrested needs revived in the transference, it is inevitable that the therapist will "fail" the patient, and that under such circumstances borderline symptoms may appear. In our experience, it is only when the subjective validity and meaning for the patient of these disjunctions and selfobject failures go chronically unrecognized and unanalyzed (often because they threaten the therapist's self-organization requirements), and the reestablishment of the therapeutic bond is thereby prevented, that borderline phenomena become encrusted into what has been described as a "borderline personality organization." This formulation of borderline symptomatology illustrates the general psychological principle that psychopathology cannot be understood psychoanalytically apart from the intersubjective contexts in which it arises and recedes.

9

Treatment of Psychotic States

> If there is one lesson that I have learned during my life as an analyst, it is the lesson that what my patients tell me is likely to be true—that many times when I believed that I was right and my patients were wrong, it turned out, though often only after a prolonged search, that *my* rightness was superficial whereas *their* rightness was profound.—*Kohut (1984, pp. 93–94)*

From our efforts to formulate the basic theoretical constructs for a psychoanalytic science of human experience two fundamental ideas have crystallized as central guiding principles. One, the concept of an intersubjective field, has been the primary organizing focus of this book. The idea of a system of differently organized, interacting subjective worlds has been shown to be essential for comprehending both the vicissitudes of psychoanalytic therapy and the process of human psychological development. The second fundamental idea is the concept of *concretization*—the encapsulation of organizations of experience by concrete, sensorimotor symbols. In our earlier work (Atwood and Stolorow, 1984), this concept was seen to illuminate a diverse array of psychological phenomena, including neurotic symptoms, symbolic objects, sexual and other enactments, and dreams. We believe that all forms of psychopathology must be understood psychoanalytically in terms of the specific intersubjective contexts in which they arise. A broad range of psychopathological symptoms are thereby recognized as concrete symbols of the psychological catastrophes and dilemmas that emerge in specific intersubjective fields.

Here we extend these two basic principles to the most severe reaches of psychological disorder. Our aim is to show how the concepts of intersubjectivity and concrete symbolization illuminate the origins, meanings, and functions of psychotic states and how, through this new understanding, psychotic patients can become accessible to psychoanalytic treatment.[1] We begin by presenting a schematic outline of our conceptualization of psychotic states and their treatment.

SCHEMATIC CONCEPTUALIZATION OF PSYCHOTIC STATES AND THEIR TREATMENT

1. Essential to the structuralization of a sense of self is the acquisition of a firm belief in the validity of one's own subjective experiences. The early foundations of this belief are consolidated through the validating attunement of the caregiving surround to the child's perceptions and emotional reactions. When such early validating responsiveness has been consistently absent or grossly unreliable, the child's belief in his own subjective reality will remain unsteady and vulnerable to dissolution—a specific structural weakness that we regularly find as predisposing to psychotic states in later life.

2. The *intersubjective context* in which psychotic states take form can be formulated in the following general terms: A person with the structural weakness just described encounters a triggering situation that evokes both a powerful emotional reaction and an urgent need for a response from an object that would validate the subjective reality of the experience. When this validating response is not present, replicating the faulty attunement of his childhood surround, then his belief in his own psychic reality cannot be sustained, his affective reaction cannot be integrated, and he is threatened with impending fragmentation.

3. In a desperate attempt to maintain psychological integrity, the psychotic person elaborates delusional ideas that *symbolically concretize* the experience whose subjective reality has begun to crumble. The concrete delusional images serve to dramatize and reify his endangered psychic reality, casting it in a material and substantial form, thereby restoring his vanishing belief in its validity. Inchoate terror, for exam-

---

[1]In earlier, valuable contributions, Magid (1984), Trop (1984), and Hall (1984/85) have shown that the use of a self psychological approach can enhance the psychoanalytic treatability of psychotic patients. Josephs and Josephs (1986) have arrived independently at an approach to psychotic states that is similar in important respects to ours.

ple, is transformed into a clear and tangible persecutory vision; damaging intrusions, into poisoned food; disbelief, into mocking voices. Psychotic delusion formation thus represents a concretizing effort to *substantialize* and *preserve* a reality that has begun to disintegrate, rather than a turning away from reality, as has been traditionally assumed (Freud, 1911, 1924).[2]

4. Once set in motion, the concretizing process encompasses ever-widening spheres of perception, as the psychotic person strives futilely to evoke the needed responsiveness from objects in the surround. The escalation and tenacity of the delusional elaborations are a measure of the urgency of the need for validation of the core of subjective truth that they symbolically encode. When the concretizing symbols are taken literally and dismissed as madness, this only intensifies the need for validation and further escalates the psychotic process.

5. In our experience, such delusional ideas form the nucleus of psychotic states. Other symptoms represent either further, more extreme concretizations of the delusional ideas (e.g., sensory hallucinations) or defensive formations that protect against them and their accompanying affects (e.g., catatonic stupor).

6. It follows from the foregoing conceptualization that essential to the psychoanalytic treatment of psychotic patients is that the therapist strive to comprehend the core of subjective truth symbolically encoded in the patient's delusional ideas, and to communicate this understanding in a form that the patient can use. Consistent empathic decoding of the patient's subjective truth gradually establishes the therapeutic bond as an archaic intersubjective context in which his be-

---

[2]Within our framework the classical dichotomy between psychosis and neurosis is replaced by the idea of an *experiential continuum* involving differing degrees of subjective validity. At one end of this continuum lie the phenomena of psychosis, characterized by a crumbling of the subjective reality of the person's experience. At the other end, in the realm of neurosis and normality, the validity of experience is more firmly established. Intermediate between these poles, we suggest, lie a group of phenomena that object relations theorists have subsumed under the concept of the "introject." An introject, from our vantage point, is a region of invalidity in a person's experience that has been filled in by the perceptions and judgments of some emotionally significant other. This conceptualization helps us to understand why it is that in psychotic states a person's introjects so often undergo dramatic materializations in hallucinations and delusions. Such materializations serve to reify experiences of subjective usurpation, as the fragile validity of the person's experience comes under increasing attack.

lief in his own personal reality can become more firmly consolidated. Concomitantly, we have found, the delusional concretizations become less necessary, recede, and eventually even disappear, only to return again if the therapeutic bond or its subjective validating function becomes seriously disrupted.[3]

This formulation extends our earlier work on so-called negative therapeutic reactions (Brandchaft, 1983; Atwood and Stolorow, 1984) and borderline phenomena (chapter 8), in which we demonstrated that it was essential for the progress of treatment for therapists to recognize that embedded in their patients' emotional storms, enactments, recalcitrance, and escalating symptomatology were kernels of subjective truth deriving from asynchronies and derailments occuring within the therapeutic system. Before turning to some detailed clinical illustrations of these principles, we wish to offer some reflections on why analysts have so often failed to recognize or even search for the subjective reality symbolized in psychotic productions.

OBSTRUCTIONS TO THE SEARCH FOR SUBJECTIVE TRUTH

One source of interference with the quest for subjective truth is the presumption of an objective reality "known" by the analyst and "distorted" by the patient (see chapter 1). In general, we find that therapists are most likely to invoke the concepts of objective reality and distortion when the patient's experiences contradict perceptions and beliefs that the therapist requires for his own well-being. This can be seen especially clearly in the treatment of psychotic patients when the therapist reacts to the literal content of their delusional ideas (rather than to their symbolic meaning). Consequently, the patient's perceptions

---

[3]Subsequent to the writing of this chapter it came to our attention that during an interview conducted on 12 March 1981 Kohut offered some remarks on the psychoanalytic treatment of psychotic states that closely parallel our views. He said, "The borderline, with the psychoses, is a relative one. It depends not only . . . on the patient and his pathology, but also on the ability of the therapist to extend his empathy to the patient. Insofar as you can truly build a bridge of empathy to a person, to that extent he is not psychotic . . . I am calmly treating people now who are delusional . . . The delusions are in response to things felt about me and the world. They become a psychologically meaningful way of expressing states" (quoted in Kohut, 1985, pp. 250–251).

threaten to usurp the *therapist's* objectifying reifications of his own personal reality. The danger of psychological usurpation has been *reified* in the widely used theoretical concept of "projective identification," a mechanism through which patients are presumed to be able to translocate parts of themselves into the psyche and soma of their therapists.

Searles (1963), whose clinical accounts vividly demonstrate the role of intersubjective reality and concrete symbolization in the psychotic process, candidly describes his own experience of this threat to personal selfhood encountered in his work with two psychotic patients:

> [O]ne of my great difficulties in the work with this woman had to do with my susceptibility to being drawn into arguing with her delusional utterances. On innumerable occasions I could no longer sit silent while the *most basic tenets of my concept of reality were being assaulted*, not merely by the content of her words but by the tremendous forcefulness of her personality; on these occasions, the *preservation of my sanity* demanded that I speak [p. 679, emphasis added].

> I had come to experience . . . a deep confusion in myself in reaction to her forcefully and tenaciously expressed delusions, which I came eventually to feel as *seriously eroding all the underpinnings of my sense of identity*, all the things about myself of which I had felt most sure: namely, that I am a man, that I am a psychiatrist, that I am engaged in fundamentally decent rather than malevolent work, and so on . . . [p. 692, emphasis added].

As Searles also points out, therapists who feel the mainstay of their sense of reality threatened may be compelled to erect a defensive wall between their reality and their patients', dismissing the latter as madness, projective identification, or transference distortion. Therapists may also attempt to persuade their patients to admit they are mad, projecting, or distorting in order to fortify the therapist's own endangered psychological world. The resulting struggle between therapist and patient stems not from wishes to "drive each other crazy" (Searles, 1959), but from their efforts to preserve the integrity of their respective psychic realities. To the extent that the therapist is drawn into such a struggle, any inquiry into the patient's subjective truth becomes thereby precluded, further accelerating and entrenching the psychotic process.

An additional hindrance to the investigation of the subjective reality symbolized in psychotic states can be found in prevailing theoretical ideas that attribute such disorders to the operation of intrapsychic mechanisms located solely within the patient. A particularly clear example of this trend is Freud's (1911) interpretation of the Schreber case. He claimed that Schreber's persecutory delusions of being transformed (by his physician and later by God) into a woman for the purpose of sexual abuse were a product of his defensive struggle against passive homosexual impulses. Subsequent studies (e.g., Schatzman, 1973; Niederland, 1974) have uncovered persuasive evidence that these delusions are best understood as symbolic transformations of Schreber's early experiences at the hands of his father, whose abusive and autocratic child-rearing practices were aimed at crushing his son's will and coercing him into submission—subjective dangers that apparently were revived at the time of onset of Schreber's psychosis. For Freud, the path to this kernel of subjective truth was blocked by his commitment to a theory of instinctual determinism. The frequently observed correlation between conflictual homosexuality and paranoia does not warrant the conclusion that a projective transformation of homosexual wishes causes persecutory delusions. In the case of Schreber, both the homosexuality and the delusions can be understood as attempts, using different pathways, to reify symbolically a primary experience of victimization. The homosexuality that was interwoven with his paranoia can thus be seen as an eroticized depiction of a primary persecutory reality.

Not only can certain theoretical assumptions obstruct the quest for subjective truth, they also can contribute to an exacerbation of the psychotic process when they lead a therapist to make interpretations that, to the patient, indicate a lack of comprehension or a consistent rejection of his psychic reality. In such instances, the interpretations themselves are experienced as inherently persecutory, and if the therapist fails to understand this, because of his belief in the correctness of his ideas or his conviction that he is acting in the patient's best interests, then a "persecutory spiral" (Meares, 1977) is set in motion, often resulting in a delusional transference psychosis.

We have previously reported one of our own cases in which the analyst's interpretive approach eventuated in such a persecutory spiral (Atwood and Stolorow, 1984, chapter 2). In this case, the analyst's interpretations of the patient's fears of women, which were well documented in the analytic material, repeatedly confirmed the patient's belief that the therapist's sole motivation in offering interpretations was to humiliate him, lord it over him, and ultimately destroy him. Interpretations of projective mechanisms only confirmed further and inflamed the patient's persecutory vision of the analyst, which eventually became entrenched in the form of a full-fledged transference psychosis. It was gradually understood that the patient had been desperately attempting to solidify his crumbling self-experience by establishing an archaic transference bond in which he longed for his brittle grandiosity to be affirmed and sustained by the therapist's admiring gleam (Kohut, 1971, 1977). In this specific transference context, the analyst's interpretations of the patient's fears of women were experienced by the patient as mortifying rejections of his yearning for the admiration that he felt was necessary for his psychological survival. It was *essential* for the progress of the treatment that the analyst was able to recognize the kernel of subjective truth encoded in the patient's persecutory transference delusions. In the context of the transference revival of the patient's archaic longing for unconditional admiration, the interpretations of his fears *were persecutory*, because they threatened him with self-obliteration. When the analyst, over the course of several sessions, was able to clarify how, in the context of the patient's desperate need to feel admired and esteemed by him, the interpretations of fears were experienced as deadly assaults on the patient's sense of psychological intactness, this made possible both a dissolution of the transference psychosis and a beginning consolidation of the archaic selfobject transference bond.

We believe that certain theoretical ideas and corresponding interpretive stances are especially well suited to evoking persecutory feelings in the transference; namely, those that claim to discover the bedrock of patients' psychological disturbances in their inherent, unconscious instinctual viciousness.

In this connection, it was revealing to us to review the case material collected in Rosenfeld's *Psychotic States* (1966).[4] In nearly every case

---

[4]We wish to acknowledge our respect for Dr. Rosenfeld's courage in his pioneering attempts to investigate and treat psychotic states psychoanalytically. In addition, we are aware that his case studies reflect early efforts in an uncharted field. Our purpose here is to illustrate our thesis concerning the part played by certain theoretical concepts, still widely in use, in codetermining the escalation of a delusional process within a therapeutic dialogue.

presented, the patients developed intense persecutory feelings in the transference, which Rosenfeld regarded as evidence supporting the Kleinian assumption of a primary paranoid position, at which these patients were presumably fixated because of their excessive aggression and pathological splitting and projection. This conclusion seems to us to be entirely unwarranted since it fails to take into account the contexts in which the patients' persecutory feelings crystallized in the analytic dialogue. In our reading of these cases, the persecutory transference feelings regularly arose from intersubjective situations in which Rosenfeld's interpretations of the patients' primary aggression and primitive projective mechanisms were experienced as destructive, disintegrative intrusions into their precariously structured psychological worlds, thereby replicating the invasiveness of the original childhood surround.

In a particularly vivid example, a patient was described whose ability to sustain any activity seemed to be completely crushed by her mother's intrusions. Her acute transference psychosis (that is, her delusional reactions to Rosenfeld's interpretations) was characterized as follows:

> Her greatest suspicion was that I was *making her think entirely in my way*, so that she no longer knew what she had thought of before, and that thus she would *lose her own self* [p. 22, emphasis added].
>
> [T]he central anxiety was a fantasy of the persecuting analyst forcing himself into her to control her and rob her, not only of her inner possessions, for instance, her babies and her feelings, but her *very self* [p. 22].
>
> [S]he could not bear to hear me speak because, as she said, it hurt her, jarred on her, felt like an attack splitting her up into a thousand pieces, as if one were to take a hammer and hit a drop of quick-silver [p. 29].

In another context, Rosenfeld himself remarked on the possibility "that if many of the analyst's interpretations are in reality faulty and inexact, the patient's fantasy of the analyst as a persecutor may become *completely real* to him" (p. 61, emphasis added). We wish to stress once again that from the perspective of the patients' archaic subjective frames of reference, such faulty interpretations *are persecutory*.

We believe that Rosenfeld's adherence to the Kleinian theories of innate primary aggression, splitting, and projective identification led to departures from the cardinal principle that he himself recognized as indispensable—namely, that if interpretations fail to meet with success, it is the understanding that is faulty and must be revised. The insistence on the correctness of the theories in the face of continued and repetitive adverse reactions had its own impact on the psychotic transference manifestations that Rosenfeld sought to understand and explain. It precluded the investigation of these transference experiences from the perspective of the patients' own archaic frames of reference, which alone could disclose the core of subjective truth being concretely symbolized, elaborated, and communicated. When a therapist fails to recognize and clarify this kernel of subjective truth, the only options left to the patient are to accelerate the delusional process in the hope of evoking a validating response, to struggle angrily against, or to withdraw defensively from, the therapist's interpretations, or to subjugate his own subjective reality to the therapist's, leading only to pseudorecovery based on compliant identification with the therapist's psychological organization.

The following detailed clinical cases illustrate the therapeutic action of successfully decoding the subjective truth concretely symbolized in psychotic delusions.

THE CASE OF MALCOLM[5]

Malcolm was 23 when he entered psychoanalytic treatment. He had been raised in a primitive area of Mexico by illiterate and inexperienced caretakers. His father was portrayed as a swashbuckling adventurer with a violent contempt for weakness, especially in his son. His mother emerged in his memories as a childlike, inadequate, superficial woman, prone to hypochondriacal worrying. When Malcolm was three she went to New York with her husband to undergo emergency medical treatment, leaving the boy with unsupervised caretakers for two years. He had no recollection of being told that his parents were leaving or when they would return. The outstanding characteristic of

[5]We are grateful to Dr. Ernest Schreiber for providing us with the clinical material for this case example.

Malcolm's experience of his mother that gradually emerged in analysis was her absolute unawareness of or concern for his boundaries. Most strikingly, she would regularly barge into his room at any time and proceed to dress or undress as if he were not present, often without a word to him, and never with any acknowledgment that he might be reacting emotionally.

In consequence of the intrusiveness and disregard to which he was chronically exposed, a rigid pattern of distancing from others developed as his principal mode of self-protection. In college he had not a single friend nor any contact with women. His only reliable source of comfort and stimulation came from immersion in books. At 22, with no professional skills or employment experience, he settled near his parents, who had returned to the United States. His sole ambition was to become a playwright.

In the small town where he lived his life was uneventful until he began to notice the attractive daughter of a neighbor and, he believed, she him. He became preoccupied with her and wrote her a letter. He determined to put a stop to the romance before it could get started. The girl and her parents were startled by Malcolm's presumptions and called the police. The officers treated him rudely until they recognized that he needed psychiatric care. Thus began the first of Malcolm's three psychotic episodes. He was hospitalized, diagnosed paranoid schizophrenic, treated with drugs and, after some months, discharged. It was then that he sought analysis.

After several months of analysis, Malcolm completed a play. At a social gathering he was introduced to a female theatrical agent who expressed interest in his play and, he again believed, in him. Again he was both stimulated and frightened. He sent her the manuscript and became preoccupied with her. Her response was slow in arriving, and her eventual rejection was curt and businesslike. In an attempt to quiet himself, Malcolm began to write to her, his letters becoming the vehicle for his escalating pleas and demands. The more urgent his letters, the stonier and more ominous seemed her silence. Malcolm began to hear noises. Neighbors said cruel things to him and laughed at him. Messages were coming through his radio and noises outside increased in volume to hound and torture him. Threatening figures followed him or peered at him through the window of his room. He was hospitalized for a second time, treated again with drugs, and, after three months, once again discharged. If he had doubted his sanity before, the certainty and authority of his analyst in diagnosing, hospitalizing, and medicating him had now all but convinced him that he was incurably mad.

After many unsuccessful attempts, Malcolm wrote a play that was accepted and produced. Though not an overwhelming success, it nonetheless enabled him to continue the only pursuit through which he could maintain a positive sense of self. Having learned from past experience, he steered a wide course from any contact with women for a long time. One day, however, he happened to encounter a volunteer at the theater where his play was being staged. She seemed as lonely and isolated as he and, he felt, as much of a misfit. After a prolonged period in which he observed her unfailing and childlike dedication to him and his play, her unqualified acceptance of him, and especially her willingness to ask nothing from him, he began, fearfully and tentatively, to seek a romantic involvement with her.

Fate, however, dealt him a third cruel blow. He was at the pool of his apartment house when a female tenant, 10 to 15 years older than he, appeared beside him. Dressed in a tunic covering a scanty bathing suit, she disrobed with what seemed to him an obvious flair. She attempted to engage him in conversation, but he would not respond. She invited him to her apartment for a drink, and he summarily refused. It was then that he could see the angry bolts flashing from her eyes.

Now began the familiar cycle of escalating persecutory malevolence: hirelings sent to kill him, mail not delivered, poisonous gases coming through air vents, food tampered with, and, eventually, deadly neurotoxins seeping into his brain. He could neither eat nor sleep, and he began shedding weight. The more terrified he felt, the more diabolical was the torture that he pictured to make sense of his terror. He talked of doing harm to the woman or to himself. He felt an irresistible urge to flee to some foreign shore, but he could not think of a place where he would feel safe.

Throughout this period, Malcolm appeared, mostly on time, for every analytic session, even though the analyst soon became drawn into the delusional system. Since the analyst seemed to do nothing to protect him from danger and had already shown, by hospitalizing him before, that Malcolm was not to be believed, Malcolm could only conclude that the analyst must be a silent partner in the plot against him. Thus, the office became wired and every movement and facial mannerism became suspect. For a time Malcolm would produce nothing but silence or, under duress, his name, date of birth, and serial number.

The dilemma for the analyst became ever clearer and more distasteful. He could not validate his patient's persecutory perceptions without, he believed, playing into and fueling the psychosis. Yet his failure to do so continually confirmed for Malcolm that he was incurably mad or that the analyst was part of the plot. When the analyst tried to reassure Malcolm that he was not in danger or to offer alternative explanations, and especially when Malcolm sensed that the analyst was thinking that he should again be hospitalized and treated with drugs, then Malcolm's delusions would grow markedly more florid and his insistence on his own perceptions more unyielding.

The turning point in stemming this persecutory spiral occurred when, after considerable supervisory consultation, the analyst recognized the absolute necessity that he somehow decenter from his own structuring of Malcolm's reality and from his own fears of joining the patient in his "madness." When the analyst was able to desist from trying to persuade Malcolm to accept *his* reality, he could begin to understand what his patient had desperately needed throughout his life—the presence of someone who could comprehend and affirm the validity of his perceptual reality. It was then that the analyst could grasp, and interpret, the kernel of subjective truth that had been symbolically elaborated in Malcolm's persecutory delusions: the sexual intrusiveness of the woman at poolside, which replicated critical pathogenic experiences with his mother, and his terrifying recognition of the woman's hurt and the vindictiveness in her eyes when he rejected her. Most important, the analyst was able to interpret Malcolm's urgent need for him to confirm, with conviction and without hesitation, the validity of that frightening poolside impression, irrespective of how it had subsequently become elaborated. Without this vitally needed confirmation, the analyst could now explain, Malcolm's belief in his own sense of reality, in his sanity, and, indeed, in his very existence had begun to dissolve, just as it had in countless early experiences with a mother who so often was oblivious to his presence and his emotional states. As Malcolm came to believe that these interpretations were not a new ploy to disarm him, his persecutory delusions subsided and then disappeared within a period of three weeks.

Threats to the sense of reality can be concretely symbolized in images of irreversible damage to the brain. This was the danger that Malcolm was desperately trying to communicate in his delusion of the deadly neurotoxins—an archaic experience of damage that he was attempting to rework in analysis. During the months that followed the dissolution of his persecutory delusions, a memory gradually crystallized that seemed to encapsulate the most irradicable scars of his early formative years—a memory of himself as a child, believing that he was in mortal danger and crying out for help, only to draw the mocking, leering response, "How *could* you think anything like that? That's crazy!" It was this early experience, and countless others like it, that had been inadvertently revived by the analyst, codetermining the patient's accelerating transference psychosis. Now Malcolm had at last found in the analytic bond an intersubjective context in which archaic subjective truths could be recognized and affirmed and his brittle belief in his own personal reality could gradually become consolidated.

THE CASE OF JANE

Our next example concerns a 27-year-old hospitalized patient who, at the time she entered treatment, had been experiencing episodes of psychosis for several years. Jane's initial contact with her analyst came shortly after a bitter argument between her and one of the hospital attendants. When asked why she had become so upset, she angrily replied that it was "all the fault of the Catholic Church," which, according to her, had never fully recognized "the human side of Jesus Christ." She argued that Jesus was human and real, and not just a deity, and furthermore that his "human realness" had been neglected in the teachings of Catholicism, which emphasized instead his perfect spiritual nature. She intended to bring this fact to the attention of the world and personally correct the historical one-sidedness of Catholic theology. Jane's affirmations of the reality of Jesus Christ as a human being were associated with her conviction that she was the earthly embodiment of the Holy Spirit. As a member of the Holy Trinity, she pictured herself as a channel through which God's love was being miraculously transmitted to the strife-torn, suffering world. She also claimed to be personally acquainted with God the Father and God the Son, who she said were incarnated in two individuals living in her hometown. In addition, she frequently asserted that the Second Coming of Christ was at hand and looked forward to the end of the world. In the world's final hour, as she pictured it, she and the two persons just mentioned were to undergo a glorious ascension into the Holy Trinity and participate in eternal life.

In what follows, we first trace the course of certain events during Jane's childhood and adolescence, with the aim of reconstructing the meaning of her delusional preoccupations in the context of her life history. The specific incidents reviewed came to be understood in the long course of her treatment as pivotal in shaping her psychological development. In the second section we discuss how a decoding of the subjective truths symbolized in her religious delusions was essential in establishing a therapeutic bond with her.

Historical Background

The patient's immediate family circle included only her mother and two older brothers. Jane's father had killed himself when she was 10 years old. Both parents were Irish Catholics who had met and married shortly after emigrating to America in the early 1930s. During the first period of her life, Jane was a sensitive and vulnerable child whose only relationships were with the members of her family. In the parochial school she attended, she formed no other friendships, relying instead for companionship on her more outgoing brothers. She remembered her mother as a distant and punitive figure during her early and middle childhood. There were many memories of being scolded, told to go to bed on time, and do her schoolwork, but no recall of incidents of positive interactions with her. Jane's mother, in a separate interview, confirmed that she had been emotionally unavailable during much of her daughter's early life because of feeling overwhelmed by family responsibilities and especially by the needs of her husband. Throughout Jane's first 10 years, her father was subject to severe, recurrent depressions and outbursts of unprovoked physical violence. The mother summarized her own experience of Jane's childhood with the statement, "It was all I could do to tread water and keep from being drowned."

In contrast to the tie with her mother, Jane felt extremely close to her father. In spite of his emotional instability, she experienced him as a nurturing figure who loved her very deeply. There were many memories of him comforting her when she was frightened by bad dreams, intervening when her brothers teased or fought with her, encouraging her to help him in working around the house, and allowing her to sit on his lap in the evenings when he came home from his job. Being her father's favorite provided the organizing context of central aspects of Jane's self-definition. The importance of her early bond with her father was suggested by the quality of her reactions to his periodic outbursts of rage and violence. In describing such incidents, which were always incomprehensible to her, she said, "When he exploded I felt the world coming to an end."

When Jane was 10 years old, her father's depressions grew more severe and prolonged. They eventually reached the point that her mother often had to physically force him to get dressed in the morning and leave the house for work. On one such morning, following several weeks of his apathy and inactivity, Jane found her father sitting in the kitchen, smiling and laughing to himself in a silly manner. She recalled hoping that this apparent good mood was a sign that he at last might recover from his long illness. On the contrary, he disappeared from the house and a few hours later was discovered hanging by his belt from a tree and with both wrists slashed.

The suicide was a devastating shock to everyone concerned and a source of special agony to Jane's mother, who was obliged to arrange her husband's burial in an atmosphere of deep shame. Jane only learned of it in the newspapers. Her father's death was never discussed in the home and, according to Jane's account, it was several years before his name was even mentioned by anyone in the family.

Jane remembered crying to herself when she learned of her father's death, but there was no protracted period of mourning and absolutely no sharing of feelings about the death by anyone in or outside the home. She told of how after the suicide a "dark cloud" descended on the family. Her mother became deeply depressed and spoke frequently of dying, warning her children that they should now learn to fend for themselves. Jane described her mother's condition at that time with the words, "My mother closed up like gates crashing shut." She also experienced desertion in her life at school. She recalled writing short stories for two of her favorite teachers concerning the plight of lost animals that could not find their way home. Hoping for personal reactions to the stories, she was terribly disappointed and crushed when her work was handed back with comments only about her many errors of grammar and spelling.

The absence of any new bond in which Jane could feel comforted and the meaning of her devastating loss understood left her without a foundation for surviving and continuing to grow as a person. Then a shift occurred in which the focus on her father's life and death was gradually supplanted in her awareness as she constructed from sources deep within herself a preoccupying relationship with Jesus Christ. She began to experience as literal truth the idea that Jesus enters the hearts of those who need him, and she sought in nightly prayers to bring the power of his love into the center of her shattered life. Included within the developing bond to Jesus was a sense that he expected and needed her to perform his work in the world, a project in return for which he promised her the gift of everlasting love.

When Jane was 13 years old, the tie to Jesus led her to form a close relationship to a younger girl who was suffering from bone cancer. The course of this relationship was to foreshadow many of her later experiences. She visited this girl regularly, comforted her when she lost hope, helped her carry her books to and from school, and prayed nightly to Jesus for her recovery. A secret salvation fantasy crystallized in which Jane was the intermediary between God and her friend, a conduit through which the miraculous powers of Jesus could be transmitted. This young friend's illness thus presented an opportunity for the God to whom Jane prayed to show his love in a tangible way. In spite of these efforts, the condition of the girl worsened, and when she eventually died Jane thought to herself, "Jesus Christ abandoned me." Her pain in this situation was enormous, for she had believed that if she did what Jesus wished of her, he would surely never let her down.

During the next few months, Jane reassessed the meaning of her friend's death. She entertained the idea that perhaps her faith had not been sufficiently strong and pure for her prayers to be answered. She thereby restored her tie to Jesus by a familiar means: holding herself to blame for its demise. Carrying such thoughts to great extremes, she underwent a religious crisis profoundly affecting the subsequent direction of her life. Two great pathways seemed to open up before her, one leading to the satisfactions of earthly existence and the other to spiritual development and ultimate union with Jesus Christ. Keeping her thoughts secret from her family, she chose the latter path and resolved to become "spiritually perfect," no matter what the cost. This project meant eradicating from within herself all traces of self-interest and generally dissolving all the ties that ordinarily hold a person to the mundane world of human affairs. It meant obliterating her emerging sexuality, her need for human companionship, and her enjoyment of all the simple pleasures of life. Spiritual perfection, as she pictured it, also involved acquiring the Christlike qualities of kindness, compassion, and mercy. As a way of carrying through her resolve in action, she looked forward to becoming a missionary nun and to spending the remainder of her life helping unfortunate people around the world.

After graduating from high school, she made an effort to put these plans into effect. She entered a convent with the expectation of drawing closer to Jesus Christ and attaining inner peace and fulfillment. The rigorous training and instruction she encountered there, however, were utterly unlike the union with God she had anticipated, and instead of achieving perfection and tranquility, she became deeply confused and depressed. At the end of her first year, she found herself in chaos and again felt abandoned by Jesus Christ. Her plans to become a nun and missionary were therefore abandoned, and Jane returned home to live with her mother.

She remembered thinking that something disastrous was occurring in her life during the period after leaving the convent. Terrifying sensations, which she described as "inner deadness," afflicted her, along with relentless depression and periodic outbursts of anger. Although she was now 20 years old, Jane was still unable to form a relationship with anyone outside her family, and she remained far too anxious to become involved with any of the young men who occasionally expressed interest in her. She talked over some of these matters with her priest and, following his suggestion, entered on a brief but fateful course of treatment with a Catholic counselor who worked closely with the Church. This man consulted frequently at convents and seminaries and was himself a deeply religious person. Jane saw him weekly for 18 months and, with his help, obtained a part-time job in a charity organization that was overseen by the bishop of her diocese.

Shortly after this therapy began, Jane developed great love and respect for her counselor. He seemed to her to be a very spiritual person, and their weekly meetings quickly became the center of her life. So far as it was later possible to determine, most of their time together was spent in informal exchanges touching on Jane's everyday experiences and often also on various aspects of her counselor's work in the area of civil rights and other social causes. At no time did Jane disclose her secret relationship to God, which had been the theme of her inner life, and the counselor apparently did not recognize the extent of her emotional disturbance. As time passed, she increasingly experienced him as a special person with qualities setting him apart from other human beings. She was particularly impressed with his ability to cope with the suffering of other persons and imagined that he was taking onto himself the pain and misery of hundreds of people. Sometimes it seemed to her that his compassion was without limit and that the whole world depended on him. In part because of such perceptions, Jane offered support and sympathy to him and listened patiently as he told her of his work for the Church. She also remembered experiencing a strong sexual attraction during this period, which confused and bewildered her. Jane's counselor now seemed to be a perfect and holy figure, and she was terrified to let him know about any of her secret ideas and feelings.

In a state of growing inner turmoil, exacerbated by losing her job with the charity organization, Jane one day suggested very tentatively that perhaps she should stop coming to the counseling sessions. She recalled her counselor replying, "Oh Jane, now what would I do without you?" This response added to her confusion, and she dramatically shouted the words, "Jesus Christ abandoned me!" As she recounted the episode, her counselor's jaw dropped in surprise. He mumbled something to the effect that Jesus had not abandoned her, and she walked out of his office, never to return. She could not explain why she had broken off their relationship in this way, except to say that he had seemed unaware and unconcerned that she was falling apart before his eyes. The counselor made no attempt to contact Jane after their last meeting. A few weeks later she was hospitalized in a psychotic state. Her psychiatric records from that period indicate that she made statements concerning the Second Coming of Christ and the mystery of the Holy Trinity. Thus began the long series of psychotic episodes that were to disrupt her life over the next several years.

The delusions that appeared during this period never became fully systematized, but rather remained loosely organized and interconnected. Jane identified herself with the Holy Spirit, her former counselor with Jesus Christ, and the bishop for whom she had worked with God the Father. She also anticipated the Second Coming of Christ and looked forward to the end of the world. On the Day of Judgment she was to be elevated into the Holy Trinity, along with her former counselor and the bishop. Sometimes she was overwhelmed by a feeling of great inner holiness and awaited a proclamation from Rome that she had been declared a saint. On one occasion she imagined she was flying through space to Rome, where she planned to sit on the lap of the Pope. On the other hand, she also frequently thought the bishop was about to be elected pope by the College of Cardinals.

Though still a virgin, Jane entertained the idea that she was pregnant and once told a psychiatrist she had experienced sexual intercourse with Jesus Christ. At other times she implied that she had been impregnated by the Holy Spirit. She often claimed to be experiencing an immense pain of some kind, sometimes linking this pain to the feeling that she had been abandoned by Jesus Christ. She also spent a great deal of time painting during this period when she was in and out of psychiatric hospitals. Her paintings were chiefly concerned with religious themes—the Crucifixion, the Resurrection, and the Holy Virgin—but there were other recurring images of the world being torn apart, roses dripping with blood, and vivid representations of fire with the words, "I AM PAIN," "I AM ANGER," or simply, "I AM," scrawled across the canvases in large capital letters. Obviously, these ideas and images were confused and even contradictory at a number of points. There was, nevertheless, unity and coherence in the way in which they expressed the themes of Jane's life. Let us now consider the subjective truths symbolically encoded in Jane's delusions and describe how an understanding of these truths aided in the conduct of her psychotherapy.

The Delusions and the Course of Psychotherapy

The psychotherapeutic approach taken in this case initially consisted in building a relationship that the patient could experience as concretely real and reliably available. Jane at that time seemed to be more involved with the products of her imagination than with any of the people living around her. She gave her new analyst the impression that for her the world of other human beings did not really exist. In the beginning, he did not respond directly to any of the voluminous religious material that she expressed but tried instead to shift the focus of the sessions to more concrete aspects of their interactions. In addition to spending many hours simply listening to all she said, the analyst engaged her in conversations about her physical appearance, discussed her daily activities in the hospital, and encouraged her to participate with him in various art projects. Jane was never disturbed by these interventions and, in fact, seemed to enjoy them more than when her therapist tried to follow the streaming of her religious fantasies. Engaging in a direct dialogue concerning her delusions seemed impossible, for such conversation led her invariably to experience disorganizing feelings of excitement and Godlike power.

Although the concrete interventions of her therapist seemed to serve as a means of establishing rapport with the patient, they bypassed the central core of her religious preoccupations and thus were not sufficient to bring her out of her psychotic state. One idea in particular that seemed to gather strength over the first months of treatment was what Jane described as "my plan to reach my gold." The word "gold," it was later understood, condensed the two words "goal" and "God," expressing the idea that the goal of her striving was precisely to become one with God. It is also worth mentioning that Jane experienced occasional visitations by Jesus Christ through dazzling flashes of *golden* light. Her plan entailed a program of meditation and prayer that she believed would exert a peace-making force on the world and ultimately bring about the Second Coming of Christ. "Reaching my gold" meant being lifted up into the Holy Trinity.

The first time that her analyst expressed reservations about this plan, Jane forcefully denounced him for trying to interfere with her sacred mission on earth. She asserted in loud, commanding tones that if the analyst wanted to be a part of her life, he was obliged to participate in her plan and follow all her instructions regarding it. One such instruction was for him to immediately telephone her beloved former counselor and arrange for her to meet with him. She imagined this meeting as the first step toward bringing an age of eternal peace and tranquility to the human race. The meeting was also to be a prelude to her ascension into the Holy Trinity.

It was now dramatically clear that Jane had experienced the analyst's reservations about her plan as a threat to the organization of her world and that it was in response to this threat that she resurrected the tie to the counselor. In retrospect, though not recognized at the time, it seems likely that Jane had already perceived her new analyst's initial failure to respond to her religious preoccupations, along with his efforts to shift her attention to other matters, as a turning away from her reality and an imposition of his own. This repeated the trauma she had experienced when her adored former counselor turned abruptly away after she had opened her secret world to him. It is possible, looking back, that the disorganizing feelings that developed in response to her analyst's occasional direct comments on what he saw as delusions were the result of her sensing that his remarks were threatening to the constructions in which her last remaining hopes were then embedded. The expressions of Godlike power that ensued at such times, and the archaic longings for and delusions of merger with God, were, in all likelihood, urgent compensatory efforts to restore these structures in the face of the assault she was experiencing. It seems possible that had the analyst been able to comprehend this unfolding intersubjective situation and to communicate this understanding to the patient, the delusional spiral might have been averted.

It was through the eventual understanding of Jane's efforts to involve her therapist in the enactment of her delusional plan that he finally recognized the implicit truths symbolized in her religious fantasies. His perception of these subjective truths in turn enabled him to adopt a stance with his patient that was responsive to her deepest needs. He grasped Jane's plan to achieve union with God through ascension into the Holy Trinity as a symbolization in religious images of her need to rematerialize a bond to a loving paternal figure, a need that had dominated her life since the time of her father's suicide. The tie to the father, it will be recalled, was the principal medium within which Jane's early self-definition crystallized. The circumstances and aftermath of his death presented her not only with the loss of a central selfobject tie, but also with the *invalidation* of her whole historical experience of their relationship. This invalidation arose first out of his implicit rejection of her in his willful act of suicide and, next, out of the family's relegation of the father after his death to the effective status of someone who had never been. The loss of the father, followed by the family's turning away from his life and death, together with the covert demand that she also renounce her tie to him, provided the specific context for Jane's first secret ruminations on the figure of Jesus Christ. Her embracing Jesus may therefore be viewed as an effort to preserve a remnant of the shattered and invalidated selfobject bond by encapsulating it within the symbols of the Catholic faith. The subjective truth inherent in Jane's delusional linking of herself to Jesus Christ was that the very substance of her being had been, and continued to be, bound up in the connection she had felt between herself and her beloved father. Later assertions that she had been abandoned by Jesus Christ equally reflected core truths of her existence, for such claims gave tangible form to the devastating experiences of desertion she had endured at the hands of her father, her family, her teachers, and her first counselor as well.

Jane's demand that contact be established with her counselor, the man whom she identified as the incarnation of Christ on earth, expressed once again her need to resurrect and concretize the lost prior selfobject bond, following her experience of her analyst as someone who was once again requiring repudiation of this vital tie. Her increasingly desperate efforts to involve her new therapist in the enactment of her delusional plan was understood as an urgent communication of her need for a different kind of response from *him*. He had never considered or observed the effect on her of his persistent efforts to redirect their conversations toward the concrete aspects of their interactions. Now, however, he realized that she required a more powerful intervention, one that would establish the possibility of rematerializing the lost and deeply longed-for selfobject bond *within the transference*, rather than solely within her delusions. He also understood that his failure to comprehend the meaning of her urgent demands for help with her plan was being experienced by her as a new abandonment, repeating and magnifying the long history of abandonments that had so catastrophically affected her life. This could only further entrench the delusions that encapsulated both the history of desertion and her unmet archaic longing.

Bearing these general ideas in mind, Jane's analyst adopted a different strategy at their next meeting. Rather than allowing her to continue speaking of her religious plans and her goal of meeting with her old counselor, he stopped her from talking and insisted that for once she was to listen to what he had to say. He stated unequivocally that there was to be no meeting with her former counselor. He told her that he was bringing a new plan into operation, a plan in which she would become well again and return to live with the people who loved her. He added emphatically that he was himself the only person in this world she should be concerned about seeing, for it was in their work together that the goal of this new plan would be attained. In spite of Jane's initial resistance to these ideas, the analyst firmly insisted that she understand what he was communicating to her. She finally objected no more and began to cry. For perhaps 20 minutes she sat quietly in tears and then thanked him and ended her appointment.

The analyst's new understanding of Jane's need for him to assume a central place in her world marked the turning point of the therapeutic relationship and was followed by a dramatic diminution of her religious preoccupations in favor of a renewed interest in the actual persons of her social world. To Jane, the therapist's changed stance dramatized his understanding of her deepest longings and needs, and she responded by forming a profound idealizing relationship with him. Each day she brought paintings and other gifts, and when she was upset he became the only person who could console her. There were, to be sure, many times during the period after Jane's initial improvement when she would again begin to dwell on the figure of Jesus Christ and her own special place in the Holy Trinity. This occurred primarily when the new bond that had been established was threatened or temporarily disrupted, for example during separations. She constantly feared and anticipated desertion and reacted in the early stages to even brief interruptions in their work as if the fragile bond connecting them had been completely ruptured, as it had been with her father. At such times it was necessary for her analyst to resume their frequent contacts and reaffirm his new and more active stance in the therapeutic relationship. As the bond was in each instance reestablished, the delusional concretizations receded and the progress of Jane's recovery continued.

After some months, during which the idealizing selfobject transference bond seemed to be stabilizing, Jane's mixed feelings of deep sadness and rage focused on her father began to emerge in the therapeutic sessions. Until this time Jane had been more concerned with Jesus Christ than with her father and in discussing his suicide spoke only of how badly her mother had been injured. But now, with the increasing understanding of the devastating truths symbolized in her religious delusions and the concomitant restoration of the severed tie to her father within the therapeutic transference, she was able for the first time to become furious at her father for deserting her, and her hostility alternated with expressions of profound grief and loss. Having found a validating intersubjective context in the therapeutic relationship, Jane began a mourning process that had been blocked nearly 20 years before and, at the same time, revivified the archaic bond that would enable her to resume the arrested process of her own psychological development.

THE CASE OF ANNA

Anna, a 19-year-old woman who had been deeply psychotic for several years, entered treatment following her transfer from a residential school for emotionally disturbed adolescents to an inpatient psychiatric hospital. She introduced herself to her analyst with the words, "Doctor, I turn into anyone I meet. You won't let that happen, will you?" This danger seemed to materialize many times in the initial sessions, when she began to call herself by her analyst's name and refer to him using her own.

The patient's experiences of self–object confusion pertained most fundamentally to her inability to maintain her own viewpoint and resist being overpowered by the perceptions and expectations of other people. She was perpetually vulnerable to being swept into others' perspectives on herself and her situation and in the process was always losing a sense of who she was and of what she felt was true and real. The theme of vulnerability to self–object confusion and self-loss, introduced by Anna as her first communication to her therapist, came to be understood in the long course of her treatment as the central issue of her life.

What follows is an account of certain events that took place during the first year of Anna's treatment. This was the period during which the scope and significance of her many delusions were clarified and the foundations of a therapeutic bond were formed. The discussion is organized around a series of impasses that developed during the early stages of the analytic work. Each of these impasses involved specific communications from the patient that were repeated again and again, communications that initially seemed to her analyst to defy understanding and to obstruct the development of the therapeutic dialogue. In each instance, Anna's communications were finally understood as efforts to concretize symbolically, and thereby articulate, the most central subjective truths of her world. Our account focuses on the effect of the analyst's comprehension of Anna's statements on her struggle to crystallize and maintain a steady sense of her own selfhood. Information concerning the life-historical background of the patient's difficulties is also included in the discussion.

The First Impasse

Anna's first words to her analyst, as noted earlier, were to the effect that she "turned into" anyone she met. She presented this transformation as something both inevitable and terrible and made it clear that she desperately wanted her therapist to prevent it from occurring. Anna's extreme vulnerability to self–object confusion rendered ordinary conversation with her quite impossible during this early period. She could make an apparently reasonable beginning by answering a concrete question or two, but after only a few sentences she began to call her analyst by her own name, refer to herself by his, and repeat various things he had said to her shortly before. Then, noticing that there had been an exchange of roles and names, she would say, "No, you're Anna, I'm George . . . No, I am George, I am Anna . . . Are you George? . . . Am I Anna? . . . " Such comments and queries would finally trail off into an inaudible talking to herself without any clarification having taken place. These incidents, which occurred frequently during the early sessions, reflected the patient's inability to experience a consistently differentiated identity of her own. The exchanges of viewpoints also appeared to be symbolized in a series of nightmares she reported at the time. In these dreams she found herself inside a transparent globe. She was looking out across an expanse of space at another globe. Suddenly she was within the second globe looking back at the first one, and then she began to shift back and forth between the two in a terrifying sequence of inceasingly rapid transpositions.

Anna's therapist first responded to her episodes of confusion by encouraging various activities in which they could participate without undergoing the mergers and identity-reversals that otherwise occurred. He joined with her in her favorite pastimes of drawing and painting, spent many hours reviewing poetry she brought to their meetings, and listened as she played her guitar and sang. The first impasse arose after several such sessions, when Anna began to repeat the words, "Hit me." Although she had initially been willing to participate in various activities with her analyst, now the meetings were increasingly dominated by her asking to be struck. She repeated these words to other hospital staff members as well. An odd-looking grin accompanied each of Anna's requests to be hit, and the incongruity between what she said and how she looked as she said it appeared bizarre and incomprehensible to everyone she approached. There was no humor or joy in that masklike expression, and if asked why she smiled, she invariably answered, "Hit me."

The therapeutic sessions eventually came to consist almost exclusively of going around in circles about Anna's ever-renewed requests to be struck. The meetings would begin when she responded to her analyst's greeting by saying, "Hit me." She then often came over to his chair, sat down on the floor before him, and softly intoned the words, "Hit me, hit me, hit me." However he responded, these same words were repeated, and when the session was over and she was preparing to leave, she always turned for a last look into his eyes and said, "Hit me."

Anna's therapist was not immediately able to fathom the meaning of her requests. When he asked her why she wanted to be hit, she replied simply, "Hit me." If he voiced his own ideas about what might underly her constant requests, she answered only with those same two words. He tried, for example, to explore the many things that could conceivably make Anna feel she deserved to be struck. She always responded to these attempts by asking to be hit. He suggested that perhaps she believed it inevitable that he would strike her and rather than wait passively for her fate, she was choosing to bring the anticipated blows on herself. She answered, "Hit me." Speculating on the meaning of her requests, he once suggested she might be feeling that her very existence was a crime of some sort and that she should be punished just for being alive, occupying space, and taking up anyone's time. She replied, as always with that peculiar half-smile, "Hit me."

Finally, during one of their many meetings dominated by this issue, when all communication seemed to have ceased, the therapist interrupted Anna's repetitious request by telling her to write rather than speak. He added that he would answer in the same way. This intervention was based on the idea that perhaps there was something about speaking in a face-to-face encounter that made it impossible for Anna to express what she felt. It was hoped that the less direct medium of written communication might permit her to tell more of what she was experiencing. The first words Anna wrote on the paper her analyst provided were, "Hit me." He then wrote back, "Why do you want me to hit you?" She responded, again in writing, "Hit me." Then he wrote, "I don't want to hit you." Once more she scribbled on the page, "Hit me." At this point her analyst wrote, "I don't want to cause you pain." For the very first time she answered him differently, by printing in small letters in the upper corner of the paper, "Physical pain is better than spiritual death." Simultaneously, as she looked at him, the bizarre half-smile disappeared and was replaced by a facial expression in which he believed he saw immense despair.

Anna's requests to be struck were now comprehended as concrete symbolizations of her need to feel enlivened by the impact of her analyst's presence in her world. They were efforts to bridge the divide separating him from an alienated inner self that otherwise could be experienced only as emptiness and death. It was now clear that the activities encouraged by the therapist during the initial phase of therapy had failed to make contact with this deeply isolated inner self and that in asking to be hit she was communicating her longing for this absent contact. The urgency of her requests reflected her escalating terror that he would never be able to recognize his lack of connection with her.

The poetry Anna continued to bring to the sessions also made reference to her deathlike mode of being. A special feature of her subjective states was that they seemed to be occurring within a central part of her that she felt had never been perceived by other human beings, a part that she viewed as the true essence of her own self. She was subject within this inner region to a powerful sense of isolation, estrangement, and ultimately doubt as to her very existence. The following extract from her writing, composed years before her transfer to the hospital, gives expression to some of these feelings.

it all came down on me
so i hid in my special closet
but no one was around
to report me missing . . .
i am looking for my soul
in an empty corridor of my mind . . .
empty is my soul
alone am i
only can i exist
like a dead piece of wood.

After Anna's "spiritual death" had been disclosed and understood, she never again asked to be hit. She remained vulnerable nevertheless to recurring episodes of numbing depersonalization, especially during periods of separation from her analyst. Even the interval of one or two days between their sessions became unendurable torture to her, threatening to plunge her back again into deathlike isolation and emptiness. During an early separation lasting one week, she made numerous slashing cuts on her arms and chest with a stolen razor blade. The experience underlying this behavior, she later explained, had been an indescribably terrible "loss of all feelings." By inflicting pain on herself and causing her blood to flow from the cuts, she had been trying to "feel again" and return from death to life.

During subsequent meetings, Anna began to verbalize directly the felt absence of her own self. She repeatedly said, "I'm not alive," "I don't exist," "I have no self." She also often cried out the words, "I'm not here, I'm not here!" Once she characterized herself as a "cavity in the world." These statements expressed her experience of herself as insufficient, absent, a nonbeing. Her analyst, recognizing that these negative descriptions embodied her efforts to articulate and convey what she authentically felt, sought to reinforce the bond that was developing between himself and his patient by communicating in all the ways at his disposal his understanding of what she expressed. Reactions of acknowledgment and understanding on his part always seemed to calm and reassure her.

The Second Impasse

After the resolution of the impasse brought about by Anna's asking to be struck, a new theme began to appear in her conversation. This was the idea that there were things she called "blocks" and "walls" located inside of her. The notion of "blocks" was associated with an elaborate delusional system that she revealed in discussions of secret meditations she had been practicing for two years. She claimed these meditations helped her "dissolve and break down tremendous numbers of blocks and walls." A leap of extraordinary progress in this "dissolving" had taken place, according to her account, just prior to her transfer from the residential school to the hospital. She said she had ceased speaking for a full two months and devoted all her energies to "dissolving the blocks and walls" that afflicted her. The final goal of her efforts, to be achieved with the elimination of the last "block" or "wall," was to undergo a transformation she described as "becoming born." The goal of being "born" contained for Anna all that seemed worthy of pursuit in life. She visualized it as reaching a pinacle of human development, a nirvana-state beyond the capacity of ordinary people to attain or even imagine attaining.

The chief obstacle to "birth" resided in the "walls" and "blocks" that needed constantly to be broken down. Through many conversations with the analyst it gradually became clear that a "block," as she thought of it, was the result of an act of psychic violence against her by other persons. She specifically pictured this act as a ray or vibration of some sort emerging from a hostile person's eyes, traversing space and striking her face, and then sinking through the layers of her skin and penetrating the surface of her brain. The final stage in this persecutory assault was the depositing of a tangible substance, referred to alternately as a "wall" or a "block," deep within her neural tissues. In a discussion of these matters Anna once drew a picture of a person's head showing such a "block" interposed between a darkened region at the center of the brain and the face. Near the darkened area at the brain's center she wrote the words "soul-cave" and "heart-cave," while the face was given the label "the dead surface." This diagram was actually a self-portrait, exhibiting the divided structure of Anna's self-experience.

The "dead surface," a term often appearing in Anna's conversations, referred sometimes to her face and sometimes to her whole physical body. The idea was that her visible embodiment in the world was a surface lacking depth, a nonliving mask or shield that had no connection to her "soul" or "heart-soul," which she located at the center of her brain. She also sometimes thought of this central soul-part as having a body of its own, one that could be "projected" into other places and times and into "higher dimensions" as well.

Anna's image of "the dead surface" concretized her experience of herself in her social world. The person she felt she was seen as being had nothing to do with the person she believed she really was. Her deeper and more essential self, as she experienced it, was completely invisible to other people. The being of this deeper self was in fact defined through its negativity: it was absent, unseen, unborn; it was a bit of pure nothingness, an empty "cavity" in the midst of the positively existing universe.

Anna once claimed that she had been instructed how to create her "dead surface" by "members of a religious order," and she often alluded to the presence of mysterious beings no one else perceived. These entities assisted her in "dissolving blocks" and advancing toward "birth."

She further described them as "walking" her through life, conveying the impression that they were protective spirits watching over her and holding her as she moved through the course of her experiences. Anna referred to the guardian figures with the names of real persons she had known during previous eras of her life. Frequently, during the early months of therapy, one or another of the figures assumed control of Anna's body and spoke for her to other people, including to her analyst.

The second impasse in Anna's treatment arose when her delusions regarding the imaginary protectors and the "blocks" and "walls" became manifest within the therapeutic relationship. She first revealed the existence of the protectors who "walked" her through life by telling her therapist that from the outset he had been talking mainly to them rather than to Anna herself. In a note from one of the figures, a young man known as "Tom," it was explained that Anna was terribly frightened that her analyst did not realize that he had not always been speaking to her. For a long time most of the analytic sessions were conducted by this "Tom," who more and more clearly emerged as Anna's central protector. She had once known a real person having this name and had felt deeply loved by him. In her delusion of his continuing presence she thus retained a bond with someone she had experienced as connected to the most vital part of her.

The most difficult aspect of dealing with Anna's many delusions, from the standpoint of her therapist's experience of the treatment, was when she began to accuse him of projecting the "blocks" and "walls" into her. In the beginning, she had referred to this persecution in the past tense, as if it were something certain unnamed others had done to her long before. She originally explained these matters to her analyst in the belief that he could help her break down the many "blocks" that had formed and make progress toward "becoming born." She once even told him he was her "greatest birth guard." Now, however, she said he had started "blocking" her himself and was in fact undoing the results of years of her work of "dissolving." Often during the analytic sessions, in a seemingly innocuous conversation about the events of Anna's day, she suddenly stared intensely at him and said, "You're blocking me, you're blocking me! Stop it, please stop!" When these accusations were first voiced, her analyst was not familiar with the various details of her delusions, nor did he have any understanding of their symbolic significance. When he reacted to Anna's claims by asking her to elaborate on what she had felt he was doing to her, she looked at him incredulously and repeated her demand that he immediately stop. She responded to his questions by saying, "Stop blocking me! Oh God, it's killing me! I was on the surface, but now I'm sinking. Going, going, going . . . gone!" The therapist found it extremely difficult to sit helplessly session after session, week after week, listening to Anna's ever-repeated pleas that he stop "blocking" her, especially when he could not identify the slightest aspect of his own behavior that corresponded to what she claimed. He knew she felt "rays" were flooding out of his eyes and piercing her head, but he could find no way to respond to what she said or alleviate her pain. It seemed to him that he was being accused of committing a psychic rape and murder of his patient's brain, and he finally reacted to the relentless onslaught of her claims by denying that any such thing was taking place. He said he was not "blocking" her, there were no "rays" coming from his eyes or his mind, and such things were physically impossible in any case and happened only in science fiction. Unable to comprehend her claims on any level other than that of their literal concreteness, he had begun to experience her communications as an assault on his self-definition and sense of what was real. His reaction of denying the validity of her delusions was thus brought about in part by his need to reaffirm the truth of *his* convictions. Anna's response to this denial was to lapse into muteness. For several of their meetings, a pattern was followed in which, first, Anna would tell the analyst he was "blocking" her or "making walls," he would deny the reality of her claims, and then she would become silent and turn away until their session was over.

The impasse was finally broken when the therapist recognized that a profound disjunction between their respective worlds of experience had developed. This recognition enabled him to decenter from the literal content of her delusional beliefs and seek a new understanding of their meaning in the context of her life history. The most striking feature of Anna's history, as it was reconstructed in her therapy, was the way her caregivers had consistently invalidated her perceptions and undermined her strivings for self-demarcation and autonomy. Anna's family included herself, her parents, and a sister seven years younger. According to her mother, Anna as an infant had "never nursed properly," "vomited back most of the food she was given for the first two years," and always "refused to cuddle." Anna was further described as engaging from a young age in "unprovoked acts to upset her parents," acts that over her first five years convinced her mother that she was emotionally ill. Anna reportedly reacted to her parents' first attempts to be affectionate with her by crying and turning away, as though they were intolerable intrusions. She also rebelled persistently against their efforts to discipline her and teach her distinctions between acceptable and unacceptable behavior. The mother recalled an incident from when Anna was four that typifies the pattern of interaction dominating her early childhood years. One afternoon as Anna was being dressed and prepared to accompany her mother on a shopping trip, she suddenly stripped off her clothes, climbed into the bathtub, squatted down, and urinated. Her mother remembered her looking up with an expression of "pure spitefulness" and saying, "I will piss where *I* want to!" This behavior, affirming Anna's control over her own bodily functions, was regarded by her mother as an indisputable sign of mental illness and precipitated the first in a long series of visits to child psychiatrists.

The relationship with the father was also fraught with difficulties. He was subject to severe depressions and came to rely on Anna to lighten his gloomy moods and support his tenuous self-esteem. Anna accommodated herself to her father's pressing needs, and a quasi-romantic tie serving to fend off his depressions came into being. This bond was the most important of Anna's relationships between the ages of five and ten. Her father angrily excluded her mother from this special tie. He often took Anna aside, telling her how good it would be if her mother died, since he and she had each other and that was all that mattered. At the same time, he was unable to tolerate her expressing even the slightest negative feeling toward him. He experienced such disruptions of their tie as a terrible emotional injury. On one occasion when she refused to do something he wanted and angrily talked back to him, he tried to strangle her and had to be physically restrained by his wife. During her therapy, reflecting back on these years, Anna wrote a poem describing a choice between being a "live monster" or a "dead princess." Being her father's "princess" by fulfilling his expectations and archaic selfobject needs entailed for her a psychological death produced by the cancellation of her own identity as a distinct person. Any effort to rebel against his expectations and establish a life according to her own design led her to be perceived by him as something monstrous and destructive.

Anna's family moved from one city to another eight times during her first ten years. She never developed successful peer relationships during this period and, according to her mother, was always considered odd by other children. In addition to the interference in peer relationships caused by the family's constant moves, the parents often intervened directly when they did not approve of Anna's friends. Their interventions were motivated by fear for their daughter's welfare and a lack of faith in her ability to look after her own best interests. Anna told a poignant story of her parents' breaking off one of her friendships when she was nine years old. She had been seeing a great deal of a girl her own age who lived down the block and who was inseparable from a dog her family had owned for many years. One day Anna came home with a cut on her leg. When asked how she had been cut, she answered that she had been playing with her friend and the dog. The parents then jumped to the conclusion that the cut was a dog bite. Although she protested that she had not been bitten by her friend's dog, the parents nevertheless forced the other girl's family to arrange to have their pet quarantined and observed for rabies at a local animal hospital. After this incident the other family refused to allow their daughter to play with Anna, and the two never spent time together again.

The first of Anna's psychotic experiences occurred when she was 12 years old. It was triggered by the loss of a close romantic relationship with a boy she had met on the streets. This was during a year when, for the very first time in her life, she found a group of peers with whom she felt she truly belonged. She shared their interest in rock music, adopted their style of dress and speech, and resonated deeply to their irreverent attitudes toward the adult world. Unfortunately these young people, including Anna's boyfriend, were heavily involved with drugs. Anna's parents again became alarmed by her choice of friends and especially by her experimentation with the drugs they supplied. Anticipating the terrible possibility of their daughter's life being ruined by addiction to psychoactive chemicals, they decided to bring an end to her romance and terminate all her contacts with her new friends. Although for a time Anna struggled against her parents' interference, they were finally successful and her short-lived romance was broken off. She reacted to this disruption by falling into a paranoid state. She reported hearing voices talking about her in school, accused people of "watching" her, "jeering," and "making jokes," and thought various people were secretly "ganging up" on her in a conspiracy. These experiences so disturbed her family that they arranged for her first psychiatric hospitalization. Anna's long career in mental health institutions had begun.

With the aid of this historical information, Anna's therapist was finally able to grasp the significance of her delusions. He recognized that Anna's experience of herself and her world had been profoundly invalidated and undermined during her entire development. The devastating impact of what she had endured was vividly symbolized in a dream she brought to one of the therapeutic sessions. This dream followed immediately on a conflict-filled weekend spent at home with her parents. The conflicts were mainly with her mother, who had repeatedly reacted to Anna's oppositional behavior during the weekend by reminding her she was emotionally ill and pressuring her to take her prescribed medications. Anna had experienced her mother's reactions as annihilating rejections of what she was feeling during the time they were together. The home visit thus recreated long-standing cycles of action and reaction that had been central to the genesis of Anna's difficulties. The dream began with an image of a large standing mirror in her parents' bedroom. Anna felt she was somehow looking out at the doorway from within or behind this mirror. Through the doorway walked her mother, with her father in the background. Her mother was carrying a loaded revolver. She pointed the gun at the mirror (and thus at Anna) and fired. The glass shattered into thousands of fragments, and Anna herself was no longer present. After a few moments, a disembodied voice began softly to intone the words, "but a shadow on the wall, but a shadow on the wall." At the same time, there was an impression of a faint silhouette passing quickly across the white wall next to where the mirror had stood. Her parents' reactions had shattered Anna's selfhood and reduced her existence to virtually nothing, at most a fleeting shadow, a silhouette of something indistinct.

Anna's therapist now understood that in order to feel that she had any substantial existence, Anna required immersion in a powerfully validating archaic selfobject bond. He recognized further that her vulnerability was such that even momentary lapses in attunement to her subjective states precipitated an experience of the annihilation of her very being. The guardian figures whom Anna characterized as "walking" her through her days, it now became clear, embodied her efforts to construct a holding environment that would protect her from injury and destruction. The persecutory delusions regarding the "blocks" and "walls" were also intelligible in terms of Anna's efforts to defend her own psychological existence. A "block," it was now understood, was a concrete symbol of the impact on Anna of the invalidating failures of attunement of other people. It was just this devastating impact of the *analyst's* lapses that she was attempting to articulate by weaving him into the fabric of her delusional system. She experienced such failures as extreme violence against the being of her very self, and symbolized this violence by means of the image of rays penetrating her face and depositing inert matter at the center of her brain. The buildup of the "blocking" substances concretized the transformation of her sense of inner spontaneity into the inertness of dead matter. The work of "dissolving" and the preparing of the way for her "birth," by contrast, concretely dramatized her struggle to fight back against the violence and establish a sense of her own existence in the world as an enduring experience.

It was now possible to break through the impasse that had developed in the therapy. Anna's analyst saw that his rejection of her persecutory delusions was being experienced as a new persecution, utterly foreclosing the possibility of a healing dialogue between them. When he told her there were no "rays" coming from his eyes and penetrating her brain, he was depriving her of her only means of symbolizing and communicating the destructive impact of his and others' actions on her. The denials specifically invalidated her experience of the actual fluctuations in his attunement to her subjective states and the corresponding fluctuations in her sense of the existence of her own self. The denials thus recapitulated pathogenic patterns of interaction between Anna and her parents, who had consistently rejected her experience and pressured her all her life to conform to their image of who she should be.

What Anna required, at this stage of the treatment, was for her analyst to join her as she underwent the oscillations of being and nonbeing. When she felt the annihilating impacts of his empathic lapses and symbolized them with the image of "blocks" forming inside her, she needed him to acknowledge the connection between what he had done and what she was experiencing. She needed, in short, for him to understand that he and others had indeed been "blocking" her, that is, persistently failing to understand her and support her capacity to experience the steady reality of her own being. The analyst therefore stopped denying the truth of her delusional claims and began to give a new reaction to her pleas and accusations. When she cried out that he was "blocking" her and that she was "sinking" and "dying," he told her that he was deeply sorry she was experiencing something so terrible because of what he had done. He added that he wanted her to know that he had never meant to hurt her and that he hoped they could find a way to undo the damage she had suffered. As her therapist gently spoke in this way, the penetrating rays from his eyes ceased to flow. The whole delusion in fact began to recede at this point, for now Anna was able to experience her contacts with her analyst as validating acknowledgment rather than persecution, and she reacted to his new communications by feeling restored to being. This restoration, repeated many times over the next few sessions, also had dramatic effects on her other delusional ideas. The notions concerning her work of "dissolving" and "birth" disappeared as themes in her conversation. In addition, the guardian figures no longer took any role in the analytic dialogue, which now began to be conducted solely by Anna herself. The holding function of the figures therefore appeared to be passing over to the deepening bond between herself and her analyst.

Anna never again claimed her therapist or anyone else was transmitting "blocks" or "walls" into her. At a later stage of the treatment, she even said that "blocking" was an impossibility, since no one can actually project thoughts or anything else into the inside of another person. Anna's relinquishment of her delusions, reflecting a new consolidation of self-boundaries, could occur only because the subjective truth encoded in those delusions had been fully acknowledged and understood within the therapeutic dialogue.

The Third Impasse

The third impasse in the flow of communication during the analytic sessions arose during the weeks after Anna's persecutory delusions receded. She was now able to participate in much more extended conversation with her therapist than before, for the most part staying within a framework of shared meanings and validities. There was, however, one group of new statements that she made that were opaque to her analyst, and when he was unable to respond adequately to these statements, they gradually became more frequent and eventually began to dominate the sessions. Anna asked her therapist, "Can you know my whole life?" At first he responded in the affirmative, saying he could know everything she told him and she could tell him the story of her whole life. This was not satisfactory, for she ignored his answer and repeated her question several more times. When her analyst asked her to explain further what she had in mind, she began to show alarm: "You *can* know my whole life, can't you? Do it now! I know you can do it. Please right now. Okay, go! Know my whole life!" As she said these things, she stared deeply into his eyes, waiting in eager anticipation for his response.

Over a period of weeks the therapist gathered a more detailed impression of what Anna was asking. She wanted him somehow to become aware of everything that had ever happened to her, from the inception of her life to the present moments of their ongoing contact. Nothing was to be excluded from this knowledge; no event, thought, or feeling, however trivial, could be left out. In addition, she expected him to develop this knowledge not through gradual discovery, but through a sort of blinding flash in which the totality of her experiences would be revealed to him. When he asked her if this all-encompassing, instantaneous knowing was indeed what she wanted and expected, she answered, "Yes, my whole life, at conscious, subconscious, and superconscious levels. Know it. Now!"

The therapist at first perceived these demands in terms of the supernatural powers they seemed to ascribe to him. He responded that it was not within his capabilities to engage in such limitless knowing. She rejected his answer, seizing his arm and shouting, "You *can* know my whole life. Do it! If you don't do it in the next ten seconds, I'll never speak to you again! Know my whole life. Okay, now! Ten, nine, eight, seven . . . "

Like the communications of the first two impasses, this one too was repeated meeting after meeting, week after week. Anna was unable to elaborate the meaning of the need she was expressing, other than constantly to repeat her demand. The analytic sessions became filled with the tension of conflict and misunderstanding, but without any clarity emerging as to what this conflict between her and her therapist actually concerned. Finally, her analyst told her that he did not have any idea what she was talking about and implored her to give him some further indication of how to help her. She answered, "Okay. Know my whole life. What are you waiting for? You must have some reason you are keeping me waiting. You can do it now. Go! Do it!" Each time the demands were made, Anna seemed to brace herself for something extraordinary, as if the response she was trying to elicit would produce indescribably far-reaching effects upon her. Each time, as the desired effects did not in fact materialize, this expectant attitude gradually gave way to one of bewilderment and then of bitter disappointment. Many of the sessions during this period ended with her telling her analyst to leave her alone.

One afternoon, following another of these difficult meetings, the therapist had the idea that perhaps the reason she needed him to know everything that had occurred in her life was that there was some particular thing that had happened which she could not bring herself to disclose. One way of guaranteeing that he would become aware of this specific incident would be for him to know absolutely everything there was to know. He speculated further that the hypothetical secret must have involved members of her family and somehow must represent a threat to them if brought into the open. It was characteristic of Anna never to act directly in her own self-interest if she thought her action might prejudice the rights or interests of anyone else. Dwelling on the possibility that there had been secret incestuous contacts with the father or others, or some other experiences she felt forbidden to reveal, he decided to discuss this matter with her directly. When she again began to press him to "know her whole life," he asked her if there was something important she had not been able to tell him. When she didn't answer his question, he asked her if she wanted him to know her whole life so that he would understand something she was forbidden to discuss. Again she did not respond. Then he spoke specifically of the possibility of incestuous relations with her father or some other activities she felt she had to keep secret to protect someone. With a look of shock on her face, she answered at this point, "That's crazy! My father would never do anything like that. Can you know my whole life? I know you can. Go ahead, stop waiting. Now! Know my whole life!"

Anna's therapist now began to feel that he would never understand her and that all his efforts to build a psychotherapeutic relationship had been in vain. As he waited in mounting frustration and demoralization, a shift unexpectedly occurred in his way of listening to her demands. At the time they were sitting on the hospital grounds, and she had once again begun to speak repetitiously of her need for him to "know her whole life." His attention centered on her use of the word, "whole," and defocused the rest of what she said. It seemed to him she was saying, "whole . . . whole . . . whole . . . whole . . . " It then occurred to him that if he could know her *whole* life, her life would then become *whole* within his understanding. The self she would see reflected back to her by her analyst would thus be *whole*, rather than fragmented and incomplete. This idea, in turn, helped him to comprehend her endless demands as cries for help in overcoming a profound sense of inner fragmentation.

Anna's therapist had often seen in her art the presence of fragmentation and disunity themes. In addition to the earlier drawings portraying the division between the "soul" or "soul-cave" and the "dead surface," she made many drawings and paintings of faces with the features scrambled about randomly. In these productions she often positioned one eye off to the side of the face and the other at the bottom, while the mouth would appear in the middle or at the top, and the nose was located off on the other side. Such artistic representations of her inner disarray were created concurrently with direct allusions in her conversation to a lack of wholeness and unity within herself. Once, for example, she claimed she was 13 different people, rather than just one. When queried about this assertion, she explained that one person had lived from her birth until she was two, when her parents had moved for the first time. A different person had lived from the ages of two until four, when her grandfather died. Still another had lived to the age of seven, when her sister was born. The story went on until 13 people had been described, each one living within an interval bounded on either side by a loss or discontinuity of some kind. Anna's past was not a continuous history, but rather a series of fragments having no subjective connection to one another.

It was through an understanding of this fragmentation along the axis of time that her analyst finally grasped the meaning of her demands that he "know her whole life." If he could somehow embrace the totality of her life experiences, past and present, then at the moment of that embrace the many unrelated pieces of herself would in his awareness come into connection with each other and form a whole. This was another facet of the holding function carried at an earlier stage by Anna's delusional guardians. The guardians, it will be recalled, were real people she had known during various periods of her past. She had delusionally pictured these people as ever-present companions and intimates, thereby mending the breaks in the historical continuity of her own self. The meaning of her demands at this stage of the treatment was that she had ceased relying on the guardians and was seeking to find within the therapeutic bond a means for reassembling the broken fragments of herself into a single united whole.

With these ideas in mind, the therapist posed a question to Anna the next time she made her demand. He asked, "Is the reason you want me to do this that if I know the whole of your life you might then become whole within yourself?" She immediately answered with the words, "There might be something to that." During the next few sessions the therapist paid close attention to the problem of the experience of inner disunity and fragmentation. As he communicated his deepening understanding of what she had been trying to express, her expectations of him began to change. She stopped asking him to "know her whole life" and eventually voiced an acceptance of the fact that neither he nor anyone else could provide what she had wanted. Relief from Anna's sense of being composed of disconnected fragments, as it turned out, did not depend on her analyst's literally bringing the pieces of her life together within his psychological embrace; it was enough that he simply recognized and understood the state of self-fragmentation for which she had so desperately been seeking help.

The resolution of the third impasse marked the end of the first of Anna's many years of therapy and also the disappearance of her floridly psychotic symptomatology. It was now clear to her analyst that she had been occupied throughout this first year with the task of developing and consolidating a consistently differentiated, internally cohesive and historically continuous sense of her own selfhood. Many of Anna's communications during this early period, especially the ones involved in the impasses described earlier, were efforts to evoke validating and healing responses from her analyst and others; responses she could use to assist her in synthesizing the structure of her own subjectivity. These efforts appeared in a language of concrete symbols that provided her with a means of articulating experiences otherwise impossible to portray or communicate. Once the subjective truths contained in the concretizations had been understood within the analytic dialogue, Anna was able to dispense with her delusional preoccupations and turn her attention to continuing her growth and exploring the unrealized potentialities of her life.

CONCLUSION

A specific structural weakness predisposing to psychotic states is the inability to sustain a belief in the validity of one's own subjective reality. Delusion formation represents a desperate attempt, by means of concrete symbolization, to substantialize and preserve a reality that has begun to crumble. As the psychotic person becomes immersed in a psychoanalytic process, the therapeutic dialogue increasingly becomes shaped by the patient's urgent, primary, arrested need for the analyst's empathic attunement to restore, maintain, and consolidate his precarious belief in his own personal reality. To the extent that this archaic, validating intersubjective system is established, the delusions become less necessary and even disappear. Hence, it is essential to the psychoanalytic treatment of psychotic patients that the therapist strive to comprehend and interpret the core of subjective truth symbolically encoded in the delusional ideas. As our three cases demonstrate, the prominence and tenacity of delusional ideation will vary as a direct result of disruptions of the therapeutic bond and its subjective validating function, and it is crucial to the progress of treatment that these factors be recognized and brought into the analysis. Psychotic delusions, like other concretization products, cannot be understood psychoanalytically apart from the intersubjective contexts in which they arise and recede.

References

Adler, G. (1980), Transference, real relationship and alliance. *Internat. J. Psycho-Anal.*, 61:547–558.

______ (1981), The borderline-narcissistic personality disorder continuum. *Amer. J. Psychiat.*, 138:40–50.

Arlow, J., & Brenner, C. (1964), *Psychoanalytic Concepts and the Structural Theory*. New York: International Universities Press.

Atwood, G., & Stolorow, R. (1984), *Structures of Subjectivity: Explorations in Psychoanalytic Phenomenology*. Hillsdale, NJ: The Analytic Press.

Bacal, H. (1985), Optimal responsiveness and the therapeutic process. In *Progress in Self Psychology, vol. 1*, ed. A. Goldberg. New York: Guilford Press, pp. 202–227.

Basch, M. (1985), Interpretation: Toward a developmental model. In *Progress in Self Psychology, vol. 1*, ed. A. Goldberg. New York: Guilford Press, pp. 33–42.

______ (1986), Clinical theory and metapsychology: Incompatible or complementary? *Psychoanal. Rev.*, 73:261–271.

Beebe, B. (1986), Mother-infant mutual influence and the precursors of self and object representations. In *Empirical Studies of Psychoanalytic Theories, vol. 2*, ed. J. Masling. Hillsdale, NJ: The Analytic Press, pp. 27–48.

Bergmann, M., & Hartman, F. (1976), *The Evolution of Psychoanalytic Technique*. New York: Basic Books.

Bion, W. (1977), *Seven Servants*. New York: Aronson.

Brandchaft, B. (1983), The negativism of the negative therapeutic reaction and the psychology of the self. In *The Future of Psychoanalysis*, ed. A. Goldberg. New York: International Universities Press, pp. 327–359.

______ (1985), Self and object differentiation. In *The Development of Self and Object Constancy*, ed. R. Lax, S. Bach, & J. Burland. New York: Guilford Press, pp. 153–177.

______ (1986), A case of "intractable" depression. Presented at The Ninth Annual Conference on the Psychology of the Self, San Diego, California, October 24–26.

______ & Stolorow, R. (1984), The borderline concept: Pathological character or iatrogenic myth? In *Empathy II*, ed. J. Lichtenberg, M. Bornstein, & D. Silver. Hillsdale, NJ: The Analytic Press, pp. 333–357.

Breuer, J., & Freud, S. (1893–95), Studies on hysteria. *Standard Edition*, 2. London: Hogarth Press, 1951.

Brody, S. (1982), Psychoanalytic theories of infant development and its disturbances: A critical evaluation. *Psychoanal. Quart.*, 51:526–597.

Curtis, H. (1986), Clinical consequences of the theory of self psychology. In *Progress in Self Psychology, vol. 2*, ed. A. Goldberg. New York: Guilford Press, pp. 3–17.

Demos, E. V. (1987), Affect and the development of the self: A new frontier. In *Frontiers in Self Psychology*, ed. A. Goldberg. Hillsdale, NJ: The Analytic Press, pp. 27–53.

Emde, R. (1983), The prerepresentational self and its affective core. *The Psychoanalytic Study of the Child*, 38:165–192. New Haven: Yale University Press.

Freud, S. (1900), The interpretation of dreams. *Standard Edition*, 4 & 5. London: Hogarth Press, 1953.

______ (1911), Psychoanalytic notes on an autobiographical account of a case of paranoia (dementia paranoides). *Standard Edition*, 12:9–82. London: Hogarth Press, 1958.

______ (1913), The claims of psycho-analysis to scientific interest. *Standard Edition*, 13:165–190. London: Hogarth Press, 1955.

______ (1915), The unconscious. *Standard Edition*, 14:159–204. London: Hogarth Press, 1957.

______ (1916–17), Introductory lectures on psycho-analysis. *Standard Edition*, 15 & 16. London: Hogarth Press, 1963.

______ (1919), Lines of advance in psychoanalytic therapy. *Standard Edition*, 17:157–168. London: Hogarth Press, 1955.

______ (1920), Beyond the pleasure principle. *Standard Edition*, 18:3–64. London: Hogarth Press, 1955.

______ (1923), The ego and the id. *Standard Edition*, 19:3–66. London: Hogarth Press, 1961.

______ (1924), Neurosis and psychosis. *Standard Edition*, 19:148–156. London: Hogarth Press, 1961.

______ (1930), Civilization and its discontents. *Standard Edition*, 21:57–145. London: Hogarth Press, 1961.

______ (1938), An outline of psycho-analysis. *Standard Edition*, 23:141–207. London: Hogarth Press, 1964.

Friedman, L. (1978), Trends in the psychoanalytic theory of treatment. *Psychoanal. Quart.*, 47:524–567.

Gill, M. (1976), Metapsychology is not psychology. In *Psychology versus Meta-*

psychology: Psychoanalytic Essays in Memory of George S. Klein, ed. M. Gill & P. Holzman. New York: International Universities Press, pp. 71–105.

______ (1982), *Analysis of Transference, vol. 1.* New York: International Universities Press.

Gitelson, M. (1962), The curative factors in psycho-analysis. I. The first phase of psychoanalysis. *Internat. J. Psycho-Anal.*, 43:194–205.

Goldberg, A. (1975), A fresh look at perverse behavior. *Internat. J. Psycho-Anal.*, 56:335–342.

______ (1985), The tension between realism and relativism in psychoanalysis. *Psychoanal. & Contemp. Thought*, 7:367–386.

Greenson, R. (1967), *The Technique and Practice of Psychoanalysis.* New York: International Universities Press.

Guntrip, H. (1967), The concept of psychodynamic science. *Int. J. Psycho-Anal.*, 48:32–43.

Hall, J. (1984/85), Behind the mask of the persecutor: The idealized selfobject. *Ann. Psychoanal.*, 12/13:239–263. New York: International Universities Press.

Hartmann, H. (1939), *Ego Psychology and the Problem of Adaptation.* New York: International Universities Press, 1958.

Jones, J. (1985), The concept of drive. Unpublished manuscript.

Josephs, L., & Josephs, L. (1986), Pursuing the kernel of truth in the psychotherapy of schizophrenia. *Psychoanal. Psychol.*, 3:105–119.

Kernberg, O. (1975), *Borderline Conditions and Pathological Narcissism.* New York: Aronson.

Klein, G. (1976), *Psychoanalytic Theory.* New York: International Universities Press.

Kohut, H. (1959), Introspection, empathy, and psychoanalysis. *J. Amer. Psychoanal. Assn.*, 7:459–483.

______ (1966), Forms and transformations of narcissism. *J. Amer. Psychoanal. Assn.*, 14:243–272.

______ (1968), The psychoanalytic treatment of narcissistic personality disorders. *The Psychoanalytic Study of the Child*, 23:86–113. New York: International Universities Press.

______ (1971), *The Analysis of the Self.* New York: International Universities Press.

______ (1972), Thoughts on narcissism and narcissistic rage. *The Psychoanalytic Study of the Child*, 27:360–400. New Haven: Yale University Press.

______ (1977), *The Restoration of the Self.* New York: International Universities Press.

______ (1982), Introspection, empathy, and the semicircle of mental health. *Internat. J. Psycho-Anal.*, 63:395–407.

______ (1983), Selected problems of self-psychological theory. In *Reflections on Self Psychology*, ed. J. Lichtenberg & S. Kaplan. Hillsdale, NJ: The Analytic Press, pp. 387–416.

______ (1984), *How Does Analysis Cure?* ed. A. Goldberg. Chicago: University of Chicago Press.

______ (1985), *Self Psychology and the Humanities*, ed. C. Strozier. New York: Norton.

Krystal, H. (1974), The genetic development of affects and affect regression. *Ann. Psychoanal.*, 2:98–126. New York: International Universities Press.

______ (1975), Affect tolerance. *Ann. Psychoanal.*, 3:179–219. New York: International Universities Press.

______ (1978), Trauma and affects. *The Psychoanalytic Study of the Child*, 33:81–116. New Haven: Yale University Press.

Lichtenberg, J. (1983), *Psychoanalysis and Infant Research*. Hillsdale, NJ: The Analytic Press.

Linden, H. (1983), Psychic conflict in the light of self psychology. Presented at Conference on the Psychology of the Self, Los Angeles, Oct. 7–9.

Loewald, H. (1960), On the therapeutic action of psychoanalysis. *Internat. J. Psycho-Anal.*, 41:16–33.

Magid, B. (1984), Some contributions of self psychology to the treatment of borderline and schizophrenic patients. *Dynamic Psychother.*, 2:101–111.

Mahler, M., Pine, F., & Bergman, A. (1975), *The Psychological Birth of the Human Infant*. New York: Basic Books.

Meares, R. (1977), The persecutory therapist. In *The Pursuit of Intimacy*. Melbourne: Thomas Nelson, pp. 165–176.

Miller, A. (1979), *Prisoners of Childhood*. New York: Basic Books, 1981.

Modell, A. (1976), The "holding environment" and the therapeutic action of psychoanalysis. *J. Amer. Psychoanal. Assn.*, 24:285–307.

Niederland, W. (1974), *The Schreber Case*. New York: Quadrangle.

Nunberg, H. (1951), Transference and reality. *Internat. J. Psycho-Anal.*, 32:1–9.

Ornstein, A. (1974), The dread to repeat and the new beginning. *Ann. Psychoanal.*, 2:231–248. New York: International Universities Press.

Piaget, J. (1954), *The Construction of Reality in the Child*. New York: Basic Books.

Racker, H. (1954), Considerations on the theory of transference. In *Transference and Countertransference*. London: Hogarth Press, 1968, pp. 71–78.

Rosenfeld, H. (1966), *Psychotic States*. New York: International Universities Press.

Sander, L. (1982), Toward a logic of organization in psychobiologic development. Presented at the Margaret S. Mahler Symposium, Philadelphia.

Schafer, R. (1976), *A New Language for Psychoanalysis*. New Haven: Yale University Press.

______ (1980), Narration in the psychoanalytic dialogue. *Critical Inquiry*, 7:29–53.

Schatzman, M. (1973), *Soul Murder: Persecution in the Family*. New York: Random House.

Schwaber, E. (1983), Psychoanalytic listening and psychic reality. *Internat. Rev. Psycho-Anal.*, 10:379–392.

Searles, H. (1959), The effort to drive the other person crazy – An element in the aetiology and psychotherapy of schizophrenia. In *Collected Papers on Schizophrenia and Related Subjects*. New York: International Universities Press, 1965, pp. 254–283.

______ (1963), Transference psychosis in the psychotherapy of chronic schizophrenia. In *Collected Papers on Schizophrenia and Related Subjects*. New York: International Universities Press, 1965, pp. 654–716.

Shane, M., & Shane, E. (1986), Self change and development in the analysis of an adolescent patient. In *Progress in Self Psychology, vol., 2*, ed. A. Goldberg. New York: Guilford Press, pp. 142–160.

Silverman, D. (1986), Some proposed modifications of psychoanalytic theories of early childhood development. In *Empirical Studies of Psychoanalytic Theories, vol. 2*, ed. J. Masling. Hillsdale, NJ: The Analytic Press, pp. 49–72.

Silverman, L., Lachmann, F., & Milich, R. (1982), *The Search for Oneness*. New York: International Universities Press.

Spence, D. (1982), *Narrative Truth and Historical Truth*. New York: Norton.

Stein, M. (1966), Self-observation, reality, and the superego. In *Psychoanalysis – A General Psychology*, ed. R. Loewenstein et al. New York: International Universities Press, pp. 275–297.

Stern, D. (1983), The early development of schemas of self, other, and "self with other." In *Reflections on Self Psychology*, ed. J. Lichtenberg & S. Kaplan. Hillsdale, NJ: The Analytic Press, pp. 49–84.

______ (1984), Affect attunement. In *Frontiers of Infant Psychiatry, vol. 2*, ed. J. Call, E. Galenson, & R. Tyson. New York: Basic Books, pp. 3–14.

______ (1985), *The Interpersonal World of the Infant*. New York: Basic Books.

Stolorow, R. (1978), The concept of psychic structure: Its metapsychological and clinical psychoanalytic meanings. *Internat. Rev. Psycho-Anal.*, 5: 313–320.

______ (1983), Self psychology – A structural psychology. In *Reflections on Self Psychology*, ed. J. Lichtenberg & S. Kaplan. Hillsdale, NJ: The Analytic Press, pp. 287–296.

______ (1984a), Aggression in the psychoanalytic situation: An intersubjective viewpoint. *Contemp. Psychoanal.*, 20:643–651.

______ (1984b), Varieties of selfobject experience. In *Kohut's Legacy*, ed. P. Stepansky & A. Goldberg. Hillsdale, NJ: The Analytic Press, pp. 43–50.

______ (1985), Toward a pure psychology of inner conflict. In *Progress in Self*

Psychology, vol. 1, ed. A. Goldberg. New York: Guilford Press, pp. 194–201.
——— (1986a), Beyond dogma in psychoanalysis. In *Progress in Self Psychology, vol. 2*, ed. A. Goldberg. New York: Guilford Press, pp. 41–49.
——— (1986b), On experiencing an object: A multidimensional perspective. In *Progress in Self Psychology, vol. 2*, ed. A. Goldberg. New York: Guilford Press, pp. 273–279.
——— Atwood, G., & Ross, J. (1978), The representational world in psychoanalytic therapy. *Internat. Rev. Psycho-Anal.*, 5:247–356.
——— Brandchaft, B., & Atwood, G. (1983), Intersubjectivity in psychoanalytic treatment: With special reference to archaic states. *Bull. Menninger Clinic*, 47:117–128.
——— & Lachmann, F. (1980), *Psychoanalysis of Developmental Arrests: Theory and Treatment*. New York: International Universities Press.
——— ——— (1981), Two psychoanalyses or one? *Psychoanal. Rev.*, 68:307–319.
Stone, L. (1961), *The Psychoanalytic Situation*. New York: International Universities Press.
Strachey, J. (1934), The nature of the therapeutic action of psychoanalysis. *Internat. J. Psycho-Anal.*, 15:127–159.
——— (1937), Symposium on the theory of the therapeutic results of psychoanalysis. *Internat. J. Psycho-Anal.*, 18:139–145.
Sugarman, A., & Lerner, H. (1980), Reflections on the current state of the borderline concept. In *Borderline Phenomena and the Rorschach Test*, ed. J. Kwawer et al. New York: International Universities Press, pp. 11–37.
Sullivan, H. S. (1953), *The Interpersonal Theory of Psychiatry*. New York: Norton.
Tolpin, M. (1971), On the beginnings of a cohesive self. *The Psychoanalytic Study of the Child*, 26:316–352. New Haven: Yale University Press.
Tolpin, P. (1980), The borderline personality: Its makeup and analyzability. In *Advances in Self Psychology*, ed. A. Goldberg. New York: International Universities Press, pp. 299–316.
Trop, J. (1984), Self psychology and the psychotherapy of psychotic patients: A case study. *Clin. Soc. Work J.*, 12:292–302.
Wachtel, P. (1980), Transference, schema, and assimilation: The relevance of Piaget to the psychoanalytic theory of transference. *Ann. Psychoanal.*, 8:59–76. New York: International Universities Press.
Waelder, R. (1956), Introduction to the discussion on problems of transference. *Internat. J. Psycho-Anal.*, 37:367–368.
Winnicott, D. (1951), Transitional objects and transitional phenomena. In *Through Paediatrics to Psycho-Analysis*. New York: Basic Books, 1975, pp. 229–242.

______ (1965), *The Maturational Processes and the Facilitating Environment.* New York: International Universities Press.
Wolf, E. (1976), Ambience and abstinence. *Ann. Psychoanal.*, 4:101–115.
______ (1980), On the developmental line of selfobject relations. In *Advances in Self Psychology*, ed. A. Goldberg. New York: International Universities Press, pp. 117–130.
______ (1983), Aspects of neutrality. *Psychoanal. Inq.*, 3:675–689.
Zetzel, E. (1970), *The Capacity for Emotional Growth.* New York: International Universities Press.

Author Index

Subject Index